Rockets

Rockets

STEVEN OTFINOSKI

Marshall Cavendish
Benchmark
New York

Marshall Cavendish Benchmark
99 White Plains Road
Tarrytown, NY 10591-9001
www.marshallcavendish.us

Library of Congress Cataloging-in-Publication Data

Otfinoski, Steven.
Rockets / by Steven Otfinoski.
p. cm. — (Great inventions)
Summary: "An examination of the origins, history, development, and impact of rockets and rocketry science"—Provided by publisher.
Includes bibliographical references and index.
ISBN-13: 978-0-7614-2232-7
ISBN-10: 0-7614-2232-3
1. Rockets—Design and construction—History—Juvenile literature.
2. Rocketry—History—Juvenile literature. I. Title. II. Series.

TL782.5.O87 2006
621.43'56—dc22

2005034205

Series design by Sonia Chaghatzbanian

Photo research by Candlepants, Incorporated

Cover photo: Getty Images

The photographs in this book are used by permission and through the courtesy of: *Getty Images:* 2, 50, 70, 74, 76, 83; Hulton Archive, 22, 24, 55, 62, 64-65, 88-89; Time-Life Pictures, 47, 52; AFP, 66. *Corbis:* Bettmann, 8; 16, 29, 39, 40, 42, 49, 51, 56-57, 86: Digital Image 1996 Corbis/ Original Image NASA/Corbis, 59; Reuters, 78; Handout/ epa, 81. *The Image Works:* Mary Evans Picture Library, 10, 21, 30; SSPL, 12, 15; The British Library/Topham-HIP, 14; Science Museum/SSPL, 18, 26, 32; NASA/SSPL 58. *Photo Researchers Inc.:* Novosti Photo Library, 36. Topham, 69.

Printed in China
1 3 5 6 4 2

CONTENTS

Rockets

THE SPACE SHUTTLE *CHALLENGER* BLASTS OFF ON JANUARY 28, 1986. MOMENTS LATER THE CRAFT WOULD DISINTEGRATE IN THE VIEW OF MILLIONS OF PEOPLE, MARKING ONE OF THE WORST TRAGEDIES IN THE HISTORY OF THE U.S. SPACE PROGRAM.

Arrows of Fire

Few sights on earth are as thrilling as the launching of a rocket. It starts with those few tense moments as the man in the control booth ticks off the countdown: "Five . . . four . . . three . . . two . . . one . . . Blastoff!" The engines roar, and the towering spacecraft trembles on the launching pad. Smoke and gas billow from the engines as the rocket lifts high into the brilliant blue sky until it is no more than a speck in the distance.

Rockets in space have been a reality for less than a century. But human beings have dreamed of breaking the bonds of gravity and soaring to other worlds since the dawn of civilization. There are many stories and myths about their endeavors. One of the most amusing is the saga of a certain Chinese official named Wan-Hoo who had a burning desire to fly to the Moon. One day, Wan-Hoo had his servants attach forty-seven long tubes of gunpowder to a large wicker chair. He sat in the chair and ordered forty-seven assistants to light simultaneously the fuses of the gunpowder tubes. There was a flash of flame and a loud explosion. When the smoke cleared, Wan-Hoo and the wicker chair were gone, never to be seen again. Some people who first heard the legend thought the official had achieved his dream of flying to the Moon. Others more rightly felt that he and his chair had been blown to bits. Wan-Hoo's story is probably fiction, but the tubes of gunpowder he supposedly used for his

ONE ARTIST'S CONCEPTION OF ARCHYTAS OF TARENTUM AND HIS FLYING WOODEN BIRD. STEAM ISSUING FROM THE BIRD'S TAIL SECTION SENT IT SOARING—A PRINCIPLE OF ACTION AND REACTION THAT STILL HOLDS FOR ROCKETRY TODAY.

liftoff were quite real. They were the first "rockets," and the Chinese probably developed them soon after they invented gunpowder by the seventh century or possibly earlier. The scientific principles behind rocketry, however, were first demonstrated by the ancient Greeks at least a thousand years earlier.

Archytas's Bird and Hero's Spinning Ball

The ancient Greeks were a curious and inventive people. They questioned the natural phenomena of the world around them and through experiments made many startling discoveries. One Greek philosopher and mathematician Archytas lived in the city of Tarentum around 400 B.C.E. According to one account, he carved a pigeon out of wood, hollowed out a portion of its interior, and filled it with water. He then suspended the bird from a wire hanging over a fire. The heated water produced steam. When the steam came out of the bird's rear, an opposite force was created that pushed the bird forward along the wire, so that it appeared to be flying.

Better documented is another contraption made about three and a half centuries later by Greek mathematician Hero of Alexandria. He mounted a copper sphere onto a kettle. When the kettle was heated, the water in it turned to steam. The steam then rose through two pipes attached to the ball. Two L-shaped tubes on the sides of the ball released the steam, which caused the ball to spin.

Archytas's bird and Hero's ball were little more than novelties to entertain their friends. But the scientific principle behind them is fundamental to all rocketry. The great English mathematician Isaac Newton first set it down more than 1,600 years later. Newton's third law of motion states that for every action there is an equal and opposite reaction. When the steam rushed out of one end of the wooden pigeon, a second force was created that pushed the bird forward in the opposite direction. Rockets lift off into space the same way. The force of the burning, expanding fuel escaping from the rocket, called thrust, propels the rocket upward.

Chinese Rockets in Peace and War

Steam was fine to make a toy spin or move a wooden bird, but to send a projectile high into the atmosphere takes a more effective and powerful energy source. The Chinese invented such a source probably in the 600s—black powder, later called gunpowder because it was used to fire guns and other weapons. When heated, this mixture of sulfur, saltpeter, and charcoal dust is highly explosive. The Chinese stuffed it into a tightly rolled paper tube. When they lit the tubes, they exploded, giving off sparks. These were the first fireworks. The Chinese used them to celebrate religious holidays and other special occasions.

These early innovators might have discovered, possibly by accident, that once in a while the tube did not explode. If the ends were not closed tightly enough, gases would escape and, in accordance with Newton's third law, force the tube in the opposite direction, into the air. These duds, seemingly ineffectively made fireworks, were the world's first true rockets. Soon the Chinese were using their flying fireworks for more than mere entertainment. They became weapons of war.

Two additions to the fireworks made them into viable weapons. The Chinese attached a long stick to the tube of gunpowder to direct it into the air with better accuracy. A cone-shaped nose at the top of the tube

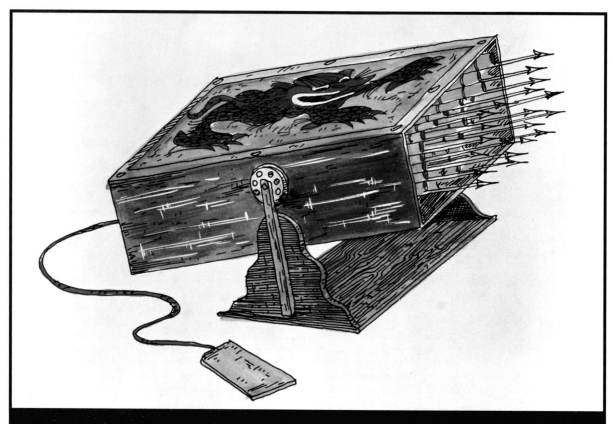

THIS CHINESE ROCKET LAUNCHER COULD HOLD MANY ARROWS. FUELED BY GUNPOWDER, ANOTHER CHINESE INVENTION, THE ARROW'S SHARPENED POINTS COULD INFLICT DAMAGE ON THE ENEMY.

could be used to store additional gunpowder and debris that on impact would explode like a bomb, causing even more destruction. According to an early Chinese history book, *The Complete Compendium of Military Classics*, published in 1045, these rockets, which the Chinese called "flying arrows of fire," were first used in battle around 1000.

These crude war rockets were more damaging psychologically than physically to the enemy. Lacking real accuracy and destructive power, they were still a terrifying sight, particularly at night, frightening and confusing the enemy as they soared through the sky.

The first historically documented use of rockets in warfare came in 1232 when Chinese troops under siege at the city of Kai-fung-fu used them to drive off the invading Mongols. The rockets must have been effective, because the Mongols later adopted them for their own defense and may have introduced them to Europe.

European Improvements

One of the first Europeans to see the importance of rockets was Roger Bacon, a scholarly English monk living in France in the thirteenth century. He made a new and improved form of gunpowder that greatly increased the range of rockets. He wrote his recipe and other thoughts in a secret code to prevent the information from falling into the wrong hands. Despite such precaution, this and other scientific experiments that Bacon conducted became public, and the Catholic Church condemned his work as sorcery. Bacon spent much of the last fifteen years of his life as a prisoner in a Paris convent.

The first recorded use of rockets in European warfare was at the siege of Chioggia in Italy in 1379. The Italians called these projectiles *rochetta* after the wooden spindles used in yarn making that they closely resembled. This was adapted into English as "rocket." Italian Joanes de Fontana designed a rocket in 1420 that ran along the surface of water carrying a torpedo that could strike an enemy ship and set it on fire.

In the 1500s, a German fireworks maker, Johann Schmidlap, built what he called a step rocket. It was made up of several steps or parts attached together that would fall off one by one when their fuel was used up. The rocket, made lighter by the loss of weight, would continue upward, ever higher. The launching of modern rockets is based on the application of this same concept.

Congreve's Rocket

British artillery officer William Congreve wrote the first book on modern rocketry, *A Concise Account of the Origin and Progress of the Rocket System*, in 1804. Congreve believed rockets made better weapons than cannons and most handguns. The recoil from these weapons, when fired, was powerful. It could injure the soldier firing the weapon or even cause a ship to capsize. A rocket's recoil, on the other hand, sent it higher and farther, potentially deeper into enemy lines.

Congreve designed several kinds of rockets based largely on those used against the British in India. He kept the basic idea of the Chinese

THESE SOLDIERS ARE PART OF THE ROCKET CORPS AND DROMEDARY CORPS OF THE BRITISH-CONTROLLED BENGAL ARMY IN 1817. THE BRITISH LEARNED ABOUT WAR ROCKETS FROM THE INDIANS, WHO FIRST USED THE WEAPONS AGAINST THE BRITISH IN THE 1780S.

A Raja's Rockets

The Chinese may have invented the rocket, but it was the Indians who transformed it into an effective weapon of modern warfare. In the mid-eighteenth century the British East India Company, a trading organization, controlled a significant portion of India. Some princes, called rajahs, refused to acknowledge the company's authority, so the British Army went to war to bring them under subjection. Among the rebellious rulers was Rajah Hyder Ali of Mysore, a city in southern India.

Hyder Ali employed an inventor who took the basic model of the Chinese rocket and turned it into an extremely lethal weapon. He replaced the Chinese cardboard tubes that held the gunpowder with tubes of iron. He also added sharp sticks of bamboo, which acted as guides and as additional weapons in themselves. The rockets weighed from 6 to 12 pounds (2.7 to 5.4 kilograms) and could travel a distance of 2,600 feet (792 meters). Special units of Indian soldiers, called Jourks, fired the rockets. They often aimed them close to the ground to inflict the most damage on the enemy.

At the battle of Pollilur in September 1780, the rajah's rockets rained down on the British troops and set ammunition wagons on fire. The sight of these fiery projectiles so unnerved the normally well-disciplined British soldiers that they broke ranks and fled the battlefield. The rajah and his son who succeeded him continued the effective use of rockets against the British until 1799.

Some seven hundred of these Indian rockets were captured by British soldiers and sent to England. A young artillery officer, William Congreve, carefully examined their basic design and conception. The samples inspired him to create rockets of his own for warfare, which he based largely on those made for Rajah Hyder Ali. The British were soon using Congreve's rockets against their enemies in various parts of the world, including the United States.

guide stick using an iron rod instead. Congreve's iron-encased cone-shaped rocket weighed 20 pounds (9 kilograms) and could travel as far as 2 miles (3.2 kilometers).

The British Navy put Congreve's rockets to the test in France during the battle of Boulogne in November 1805. But a sudden storm rendered them practically useless. In 1807, in another battle in Copenhagen, Denmark, they fired about 25,000 rockets that destroyed the city.

The Rocket's Red Glare

Perhaps the most famous rocket battle in American history was the siege of Fort McHenry in Baltimore Harbor by the British during the War of 1812. On the night of September

AN EARLY-ROCKET ENTHUSIAST IN PERIOD DRESS IS ABOUT TO SET OFF A PAIR OF CONGREVE ROCKETS FROM A BOMBING FRAME DATING FROM 1806. THIS FRAME, ALSO INVENTED BY WILLIAM CONGREVE, WOULD BE TIED TO THE MAST OF A SHIP BEFORE ROCKETS WERE FIRED FROM IT.

13, 1814, American lawyer Francis Scott Key stood on the deck of a British prisoner-exchange boat and watched as the British bombarded the fort with rockets. The next morning, however, the American flag still flew over the fort, indicating that the British had not prevailed. Key was inspired to write a poem about the experience, in which he included the lines, "The rockets' red glare, / the bombs bursting in air . . ." The poem later became the lyrics of our national anthem, "The Star-Spangled Banner."

Despite the aggressive barrage of airborne missiles, it not surprising that the British rockets failed to bring about the surrender of the American fort. Congreve's rockets were notorious for missing their mark. Beyond a certain range, they had little accuracy. In 1846 another English inventor, William Hale, improved on Congreve's design by replacing the

The painting depicts the bombardment of Fort McHenry in Baltimore Harbor by the British during the War of 1812. American Francis Scott Key watched the attack and captured "the rockets' red glare" for all time in a poem, which ultimately provided the lyrics to "The Star-Spangled Banner."

guide stick with three small fins, or vanes, along the exhaust muzzle that helped stabilize the rocket in flight and give it spin.

The United States used Hale's rockets in the Mexican American War the following year. Both Northern and Confederate troops also used rockets to a limited degree during the Civil War. But by then, newer weapons, such as the repeating rifle and the Gatling gun, were seen as much more effective in combat. The rocket, which had never been a terribly effective weapon in the first place, soon disappeared from military campaigns.

Other Uses of Early Rockets

Throughout the nineteenth century, however, people found more peaceful uses for Congreve's and Hale's rockets. Sailors on whaling ships used rockets to propel their harpoons. They positioned them on their shoulders and fired the harpoons directly at whales. Sailors also used rockets to propel rope lines to save and tow stranded ships. A rocket could carry a rope more than 1,000 feet (305 meters).

In the late 1800s, enterprising Americans and Europeans even tried to deliver mail using rockets. These experiments did not work, but they showed how inventive minds could put rockets to constructive uses. The most visionary rocketeer of all was probably Claude Ruggieri, an Italian living in Paris, France. Ruggieri believed that rockets could be used to travel into space. As early as 1806, he put small animals into rockets and sent them into the sky. The Paris authorities frowned on his experiments, and when he attempted to launch a small boy into space with a group of rockets, they finally brought an end to his test flights.

Most people of his day thought Ruggieri a crackpot. But his belief in the rocket as a viable means of traveling into space was shared by two greater visionaries in the next century, signaling the beginning of the modern era of rocketry.

KONSTANTIN TSIOLKOVSKY WROTE ABOUT ROCKETS AND THEIR USE FOR SPACE TRAVEL, BUT NEVER BUILT A ROCKET HIMSELF. A CRATER ON THE MOON'S FAR SIDE WAS LATER NAMED IN HIS HONOR.

Two Fathers of Modern Rocketry

The age-old dream of Wan-Hoo, that ambitious Chinese official who thought he could fly to the Moon in a wicker chair, finally took shape in the early years of the twentieth century. Two educators—a Russian and an American—made a solid scientific case for rockets as vehicles for space travel. Both of these men were ridiculed or ignored for much of their careers but finally received the full recognition they richly deserved later in life.

The Vision of Konstantin Tsiolkovsky

Konstantin E. Tsiolkovsky, born in 1857, was a Russian physicist and high school teacher. In 1895 he first made the astonishing assertion that humans could explore space using rockets. Five years later he published a report called "Investigation of Interplanetary Space by Means of Rocket Devices." In it and in later writings, Tsiolkovsky laid out two concepts basic to rocketry that still hold true today.

The first was that if rockets were to travel beyond the Earth's atmosphere, they would need a more powerful and efficient fuel source than a solid form such as gunpowder. He suggested a liquid fuel, composed of a blend of liquid oxygen and liquid hydrogen. Not only could liquid fuel give a rocket

Nikolai Kibalchich: Revolutionary, Rocket Designer

Russians had been designing rockets even before the era of Konstanin Tsiolkovsky. One of the most intriguing of these rocket pioneers was Nikolai Ivanovich Kibalchich. Born in 1853, Kibalchich studied at the Saint Petersburg Institute of Transportation Engineers. In 1875, at age twenty-one, he was arrested by the police for possessing revolutionary literature. He was sentenced to three years in prison and on his release joined a revolutionary organization determined to overthrow Russia's absolute monarch, the czar. Kiblalchich became the group's explosives expert, making bombs for terrorist purposes. On March 1, 1881, Czar Alexander II was killed by a bomb that may have been made by Kibalchich. For his involvement in the assassination plot, Kibalchich and five of his colleagues were arrested and thrown into prison.

During the seventeen days Kibalchich remained in prison, he passed the time by sketching and describing a kind of rocket. It was a strange contraption that consisted of a platform surrounded by a railing. A giant machine gun was mounted above a hole in the platform's center. The gun fired cartridges of dynamite that lifted the platform into the air.

Kibalchich never had the opportunity to build his strange rocket or to modify it further. He was hanged along with his co-conspirators on April 3, 1881. His notes on what is the first known vehicle powered by a solid-fuel engine were rediscovered in 1917. Years later, astronomers honored him for his role in the history of rocketry by naming a crater of the Moon after him.

the high speed it needed to break from the force of Earth's gravity, it could be held in storage chambers and pumped from one chamber to another at a certain rate to increase or reduce the speed of the rocket as needed.

The other great concept Tsiolkovsky came up with was the multistage rocket. Although earlier scientists had toyed with this idea, Tsiolkovsky was the first to elaborate it fully. He conceived of several small rockets attached together to form a large rocket, which he called a rocket train. As each individual rocket used up its fuel, it would drop away from the train. The rocket, growing lighter with each successive stage, would continue to climb ever higher in its ascent. Finally, only the smallest rocket, which would carry people, would be left to orbit the Earth. Tsiolkovsky even calculated the speed and quantity of fuel that would be necessary for a rocket to escape the Earth's gravitational pull and to enter orbit.

Tsiolkovsky not only firmly believed in the use of rockets to explore space, he also envisioned people one day living in huge space stations that would orbit the Earth. He wrote a number of science-fiction novels that described a future world in which rockets would take people to other planets. One of these books, *Outside the Earth,* became his most popular work.

For years, most Russians either ignored Tsiolkovsky's theories or thought him a bit mad. After the Bolshevik Revolution in 1917, however, the new Communist government took a serious interest in rockets and Tsiolkovsky's theories about them. The Communists funded his work and encouraged him to develop his theories further. On his seventy-fifth birthday, in 1932, Tsiolkovsky was hailed as a national hero. By then people in Russia and other countries were actually building the rockets he had written about

THE ASSASSINATION OF CZAR ALEXANDER II OF RUSSIA LED TO THE ARREST OF ANARCHIST NIKOLAI KIBALCHICH. BESIDES BEING A BOMB EXPERT, KIBALCHICH DESIGNED THE FIRST KNOWN ROCKET POWERED BY A SOLID-FUEL ENGINE IN HIS JAIL CELL IN 1881.

ROBERT GODDARD POSES BEHIND ONE OF HIS EX-
PERIMENTAL ROCKETS ON SEPTEMBER 29, 1928.
HIS ROCKET AND LAUNCHING FRAME LOOK QUITE
PRIMITIVE, BUT HIS PERSISTENT EFFORTS LED TO
THE MODERN ROCKETS OF TODAY.

for so long. In a 1933 radio broadcast, Tsiolkovsky predicted the future with surprising accuracy. "I am firmly convinced that my . . . dream—space travel . . . will be realized. . . . I believe that many of you will be witnesses of the first journey beyond the atmosphere." Tsiolkovsky, who died two years later, would not be among those spectators.

Robert Goddard— Dreamer and Rocket Maker

Robert Hutchings Goddard was born in Worcester, Massachusetts, in 1882, twenty-five years after Tsiolkovsky. As a child, he read the science-fiction novels and stories of Jules Verne and H. G. Wells and dreamed of traveling to the Moon and beyond. This boyish enthusiasm for space travel would stay with Goddard all his life.

While still a student at Worcester Polytechnic Institute in Massachusetts, he built his first experimental rocket in 1907. Goddard continued these experiments after he became a professor of physics at Clark University. His experimental rockets soared to heights of up to 500 feet (152.4 meters). After the United States entered World War I in 1917, Goddard was hired by the army to do rocket research.

But Goddard was more interested in rockets for peaceful uses, such as weather observation, than for warfare, and this focus brought his work to the attention of the Smithsonian Institution in Washington, D.C., in 1916. The institution gave him a grant of five thousand dollars to continue his work on rockets.

"The Moon Man"

In 1919 the Smithsonian published a paper by Goddard called *A Method of Reaching Extreme Altitudes*. The paper represented years of solid scientific work and came to some of the same conclusions about rocketry that Tsiolkovsky reached, although Goddard knew nothing at the time of the Russian's work. In his writings, Goddard also brought up the possibility of a rocket powerful enough to go to the Moon. When it struck the Moon's surface, he proposed that red flash powder aboard the rocket would explode and cover the lunar landscape. People back on Earth would see the paint and know that the rocket had reached the Moon.

The Moon rocket was only a small part of Goddard's paper, but newspapers and magazines seized on it as the central idea. They ridiculed Goddard as a "moon man" and a crackpot. Yet some Americans were intrigued by Goddard's theories and even offered themselves as volunteers for his Moon rocket. Fifty years later, on the eve of the actual Moon landing, *The New York Times* apologized for ridiculing Goddard and hailed him as a visionary.

A very shy and private person, Goddard was deeply humiliated by the publicity and ridicule he received and from then on conducted his experiments largely in secret. This secrecy gradually became an obsession, leading him to fear that scientists in other countries might steal his ideas if they knew of them.

On March 16, 1926, after years of countless experiments and failures, Goddard was ready to launch the world's first rocket powered by a liquid propellant. He chose a field on his Aunt Effie's farm near Auburn, Massachusetts, as the launch site. His 12-foot (3.7-meter) rocket, fueled by a mixture of liquid oxygen and gasoline, flew for 2.5 seconds, achieving an altitude of only 41 feet (12.5 meters) before landing in a cabbage patch some 184 feet (56 meters) away. Modest as it was, the rocket's short journey would change the course of history.

Rockets in the Desert

While many scientists scoffed at the brief flight of Goddard's rocket's, others saw it as the start of a new age of rocketry. Among them was avia-

By 1936, when this photograph was taken, Goddard's rockets had gotten bigger and could fly far higher. The bleak setting is the New Mexican desert where Goddard (second from left) built and tested his rockets for a decade with funds from a Guggenheim grant.

tor Charles Lindbergh, the first person to fly solo across the Atlantic Ocean. Lindbergh persuaded philanthropist Daniel Guggenheim to give Goddard a grant of $100,000 to continue his work.

With this money, Goddard moved to Roswell, New Mexico, in 1930, where he set up the world's first rocket testing site in the desert. For twelve years Goddard built and tested bigger and more powerful rockets. They eventually flew at a speed of more than 500 miles (805 kilometers) per hour and reached an altitude of 1.5 miles (2.4 kilometers). Other innovations were not far behind. These included a special container in the rocket for scientific instruments and a parachute that would open to bring the rocket and instruments safely back to Earth. This second development came out of necessity. Goddard could not afford to lose a rocket to a crash-landing or a faulty test and then have to build a new one.

Other hazards beyond damaged equipment hampered his work. They included violent weather conditions, hordes of biting insects, and accidental explosions. Once a rocket misfired and headed straight for Goddard and one of his four assistants. They dove to the ground just before the rocket could strike them.

Robert Goddard died in 1945, never knowing what the future would hold for his rockets. After World War II, the United States turned its full attention to a rocketry program for defense and later for space travel. Without Goddard's pioneering work, this may not have happened. In May 1959, the National Aeronautics and Space Administration (NASA) named its new facility the Goddard Space Flight Center. Today Robert Goddard joins Konstantin Tsiolkovsky as one of the fathers of modern rocketry.

Still, there was another legendary figure integral to the history of modern rocketry. He was a German who, with the support of his government, turned out rockets of stunning power.

HERMANN OBERTH HELPED PUT GERMANY IN THE FOREFRONT OF ROCKET DEVELOPMENT IN THE 1930S AND 1940S. A FERVENT BELIEVER IN USING ROCKETS FOR SPACE EXPLORATION, HE INSPIRED THE FOUNDING OF THE SOCIETY FOR SPACE TRAVEL.

Germany Leads the Way

Konstantin Tsiolkovsky and Robert Goddard were not the only scientists who were experimenting with and writing about rockets in the early decades of the twentieth century. Hermann Oberth, another key figure, was born in Transylvania, Romania, in 1894. Like Goddard, Oberth dreamed ever since childhood of rockets going into space. At fifteen, he designed his first multistage, solid-fuel rocket. At eighteen, Oberth independently came to the same conclusion that Goddard had reached concerning rocket fuel. He realized that solid fuel burned too slow and inefficiently to propel a rocket into space. He designed a rocket that would run on a mixture of liquid oxygen and liquid hydrogen. Oberth was a brilliant student and earned his master's degree from the University of Heidelberg in Germany. But when he wrote his dissertation on rockets to earn a doctoral degree, every major university in Germany rejected it. "I refrained from writing another [dissertation], thinking to myself: 'Never mind, I will prove that I am able to become a greater scientist than some of you, even without the title of doctor,'" he later wrote.

Unable to get his PhD, Oberth, like Tsiolkovsky and Goddard, turned to teaching, continuing to do rocket research in his spare time. In 1923 he published his rejected dissertation, *Die Rakete zu den Planetenräumen* (The Rocket into Interplanetary Space). Oberth was a visionary

Merging Fantasy and Fact— Lang's Woman in the Moon

Hermann Oberth's second book *The Way to Spaceflight* (1929) won him many new admirers and champions. Among them was the gifted German filmmaker Fritz Lang, who three years earlier had made the futuristic science-fiction classic *Metropolis* (1926). Lang was inspired by Oberth's ideas of space travel and was eager to make a film about a spaceship traveling from Earth to the Moon. He even hired Oberth as a consultant on the film entitled *Frau im Mond (Woman in the Moon*, 1929). Oberth designed a spaceship for the movie that was incredibly realistic. The entire section of the film leading up to the Moon launch uncannily paralleled the Apollo Moon launch four decades later. In the film, Lang wanted to make the rocket launch suspenseful and had a technician count numbers backward to the actual blastoff. It was so effective, that NASA later adopted the practice, and the countdown has become an integral part of every U.S. rocket launch ever since.

Unfortunately, like Lang's film, the collaboration between scientist and auteur had a less than happy ending. After the German rocket program was established, the government was afraid that the rockets in the movie were too close in detail to what their scientists were developing. Oberth's models were destroyed, and the film pulled from release.

who boldly declared in his publication that space travel was not merely an option, but the fulfillment of human destiny. He foresaw a time in the future when humans would leave Earth in rocket ships and colonize other planets.

While Oberth's ideas were exciting, his writing was not. His book was so technical that few non-scientists could understand it. Fortunately for Oberth, other writers digested his ideas and were able to express them in simpler language that the layperson could understand.

The Society for Space Travel

Oberth's enthusiasm for space rockets spread quickly, and rocket societies sprang up in Germany as well as in the United States, Russia, and other countries. The most important of these societies was the Verein fur Raumschiffahrt (Society for Space Travel) founded in Breslau, Germany, in 1927. Known by its German initials, VfR, the organization's goals were to educate the general public about the usefulness of rockets and to build practical rockets of their own.

The members of VfR were a mixed

group of scientists and amateurs. Max Valier was a tireless writer and promoter who helped develop a rocket-propelled airplane and a special rocket car propelled by rocket engines mounted to its rear. Wily Ley was a more serious scientist who became the historian of the group. Wernher von Braun, still in high school when the society started, was the "boy wonder," whose sharp mind and skill in rocket science greatly impressed Oberth and other group members.

On March 14, 1931, Johannes Winkler, a society member, launched the first liquid-fuel rocket in Europe. It weighed only 11 pounds (5 kilograms) and traveled 1,000 feet (305 meters) into the sky above the German town of Dessau.

Rockets for War

By 1930 the German Army was beginning to take notice of the VfR's rocket testing. While the society's members and supporters saw rockets as a means of traveling into space, the military saw rockets as a potential weapon for warfare. The army had its reasons. Defeated by the Allied nations in World War I (1914–1918), Germany had to abide by the dictates of the Treaty of Versailles. According to the agreement, Germany could not manufacture weapons, such as rifles and tanks. The treaty stated nothing about rockets, which were not yet developed enough to be considered effective weapons at the time the treaty was ratified. The German Army wanted to aid in that development and stockpile rockets for their country's future defense.

In 1931 the military formed a new department of rocket research under

A ROCKET DESIGNER AND A VISIONARY, WERNHER VON BRAUN'S CAREER SPANNED SEVERAL DECADES FROM THE DEVELOPMENT OF THE V-2 ROCKET IN HIS NATIVE GERMANY IN THE 1940S TO THE U.S. SPACE SHUTTLES IN THE 1970S.

the direction of a young army officer Walter Dornberger. Dornberger hired Wernher von Braun to oversee the development program. While von Braun wanted to make rockets for space travel and not warfare, he and the scientists who joined his team realized that the only way they would get the government money they needed to further their work was to develop war rockets.

A site was chosen for the testing center at the mouth of the Ems River along Germany's North Sea coast. Von Braun and his team of scientists went to work. It took them several years to develop a workable rocket. Finally, at the end of 1934, they launched two rockets that reached a height of 1.5 miles (2.4 kilometers) over the North Sea. The army was pleased with the results and gave Dornberger enough money to establish a bigger center at Peenemunde, a remote island in the Baltic Sea. The German government wanted to keep its rocket testing secret from the public and especially from other nations.

In 1933 the Social Nationalist Party, better knows as the Nazis, came to power. Its leader, Adolph Hitler, wanted to return Germany to its former glory before its defeat in World War I. But Hitler had little interest in the work of the researchers at Peenemunde. He saw little potential in rocket research and was more interested in the further development of more conventional weapons such as tanks, airplanes, and submarines.

Birth of the V-1

The first working rocket to come out of von Braun's testing program was the Aggregate-1 or A-1. A small test rocket, it blew up when the motor was activated.

By 1939 Hitler's thirst for conquest had led him to seize Austria and part of Czechoslovakia. On September 1 of that year, he had invaded Poland. Two days later, England and France declared war on Germany, and World War II erupted. Hitler's military strategy was to hit the enemy fast and hard. His blitzkrieg ("lightning war") mobilized ground troops, tanks, and airplanes in a deadly war machine that seemed unstoppable.

The initial success of Germany's war effort did not appear to bode well for Dornberger's rocket program. Shortages in liquid oxygen and in alcohol during the war made it difficult to continue testing rockets. Hitler's adviser Albert Speer showed up to observe a test of the A-4 in June 1942, but it was a dismal failure. The team went back to work and on October 3, 1942, they were ready to test the A-4 again. This time it soared a distance of about 120 miles (193 kilometers) and landed near its intended target.

Hitler was impressed with the results. The A-4 had proved that it could be a dependable and deadly weapon. It was also far cheaper to manufacture than the bomber planes the nation relied on so heavily, and no pilot was required. In the summer of 1943, under Hitler's orders, production of the A-4 began in earnest at a newly established factory in the Harz Mountains.

But the Allies, including the United States which joined their ranks in December 1941, had learned about the German rocket project and tried to put a stop to it. Allied planes dropped bombs on Peenemunde. Many rockets were destroyed, and more than seven hundred workers were killed.

THE GERMAN DEPARTMENT OF ROCKET RESEARCH EXPERIMENTED TIRELESSLY WITH ROCKETS FOR THE NAZI WAR MACHINE. A MEMBER OF THE TEAM IS FILLING THIS TEST MODEL WITH CHEMICAL FUEL FROM A PITCHER.

With its location known, the project was moved to a secret underground location in the Harz Mountains. In June 1944, days after the Allies had landed at Normandy to begin an invasion of German-occupied France, the A-1, at that point renamed the V-1 rocket, was ready to counterattack. The *V* stood for the German *Vergeltung,* meaning

IN THIS ILLUSTRATION, WORKERS PREPARE TO LAUNCH THE V-2 ROCKET, THE FIRST LONG-RANGE BALLISTIC MISSILE THAT WOULD DEVASTATE ENGLAND IN THE LAST DAYS OF WORLD WAR II. IF HITLER HAD PUSHED FOR THE DEVELOPMENT OF THE V-2 SOONER, THE WAR MAY HAVE TURNED OUT QUITE DIFFERENTLY.

"vengeance." For the next nine months, more than eight thousand V-1 rockets rained down vengeance on England, and Antwerp, Belgium, a center of Allied activities, in retribution for all the German war dead. Only a little more than a fourth of the rockets hit their targets, but they were enough to destroy thousands of buildings and kill more than six thousand people.

But the V-1 was an inaccurate missile and only by launching large numbers, similar to the barrage of Congreve's rockets in the nineteenth century, could the Germans be assured enough would find their target. The V-1 also made a strange whistling sound before it struck, giving its intended victims some warning and a chance to run for cover. The English called it the "buzz bomb."

Hitler's "Wonder Weapon"

In September 1944, only a few months after the first V-1s were launched, the German scientists perfected the far more powerful A-4. The Nazis renamed it the V-2, another tool of vengeance, but one that was far more deadly than its predecessor. It was 46 feet (14 meters) long and weighed 13 tons (11.8 metric tons). Besides being bigger and containing more explosives than the V-1, the V-2 rocket could be aimed with far greater accuracy and could move with far greater speed. It also gave no warning sound of its approach as it neared its intended target.

The Nazis fired about 2,700 V-2s at England and at Antwerp. The V-2 was truly Hitler's "wonder weapon," but it came too late to save Germany from defeat. If Hitler had taken a greater interest in rockets earlier in the war, the outcome might have been much different. But by early 1945 the German Army was decimated, the nation's cities heavily bombed and in chaos, and few resources remained to continue the fighting. By April, the Allies were marching toward Berlin, where Hitler committed suicide in an underground bunker rather than face the shame of capture.

Wernher von Braun made a difficult decision. He sent his brother by bicycle to a neighboring village to offer the rocket team's surrender to the Americans. The scientist reasoned that with Germany's fall he might finally get the chance to build rockets for space travel as he had always wanted. The United States had the resources to allow him to do that, and it was anxious to develop rockets of its own. The nearly 250 German rocket scientists who surrendered to the Americans thus were not punished for the work they performed for the Nazis. Instead, 127 of them were offered a new life in the United States and were flown to Fort Bliss, Texas, where they were put to work developing new rockets for the U.S. government.

But not all of the German rocket scientists ended up at Fort Bliss. The Soviet Union (formerly Russia), a U.S. ally, had captured some of them as their soldiers entered Germany from the east. The Soviets were also eager to develop a rocket program. With Germany defeated, these two superpowers would come to possess the world's most advanced rockets. The fierce competition, albeit ultimately for a peaceful end, would be an integral part of a new and different kind of conflict—the cold war.

THIS TOWERING WAR ROCKET SERVED AS A GRIM SYMBOL OF THE EVOLVING COLD WAR BETWEEN THE UNITED STATES AND THE SOVIET UNION.

The Race for Space

The peace and harmony that were re-established at the end of World War II proved to be short lived. Within a year, the Soviet Union was setting up puppet governments, forged in its own image, throughout Eastern Europe. In the words of British prime minister Winston Churchill, "an iron curtain" fell over the region as these countries came under the control of Communist dictatorships.

The United States soon found itself entangled in a cold war with the Soviets, called as such because it was mainly an intimidation campaign involving propaganda, heated words, and influence. To convince the other power not to attack, the two nations built up great stockpiles of both conventional and nuclear weapons. Among these weapons were rockets designated to carry nuclear bombs to enemy territory. The rockets were based on the concept of the German V-2, but would be bigger and potentially more lethal.

The United States Sets the Pace

The United States, having tapped the expertise of most of the leading German scientists, initially made the faster progress. Wernher von Braun took the German V-2 rocket and put the Wac Corporal—a small, United

States–made sounding rocket used to measure and record atmospheric conditions—in its nose to create a two-stage rocket. The army dubbed the new rocket the Bumper-Wac. Bumper was the U.S. code word for the V-2 program. The rocket launched on February 24, 1949, soared to a record-breaking altitude of 244 miles (393 kilometers), attaining a top speed of more than 5,000 miles (8,047 kilometers) per hour.

Most of the rockets that the United States tested immediately after World War II were equipped with scientific instruments to record and transmit information about atmospheric conditions and other data in space. The exploration of space was a secondary interest.

In 1950 the von Braun team was moved to Hunstville, Alabama, where the Army Ballistic Missile Agency (ABMA) would be established six years later. There, the team developed the Redstone, which at nearly 70 feet (21.3 meters) was far greater in length than the V-2. However, its limited range of 200 miles (322 kilometers) prevented it from being effective should the United States ever have to attack the Soviet Union.

The Soviets Join the Race

The Soviets meanwhile had their own version of Wernher von Braun to design new and experimental rockets. Sergei Korolev, born in 1907, was an enthusiastic member of a Soviet rocket society in the 1930s and built some of the most successful of the early Soviet rockets. He also worked as an aircraft designer. Like many military leaders and scientists, Korolev was unjustly accused of crimes against the state by the paranoid Soviet dictator Joseph Stalin in the late 1930s. He was tried, convicted, and sentenced to hard labor in a gold mine. Fortunately, he had influential friends who were able to get him relocated to a special labor camp where he designed aircraft.

After World War II, Stalin was anxious to catch up with U.S. rocket development. He released Korolev from prison to develop new and better rockets using captured German V-2 rockets as models. After Stalin's death in 1953, the new Soviet leader Nikita Khrushchev recognized Korolev's remarkable abilities and gave him the funds and necessary means to further his work, which went on in almost complete secrecy. The United States and the rest of the world knew little of what the Soviets were up to. Because the post-war Soviet economy was not as strong and as developed as the U.S. economy, many Americans assumed incorrectly that the Soviets were lagging far behind in rocket development as well.

A Missed Opportunity

In 1954 Wernher von Braun, who worked for the army, presented his proposal Project Orbiter to his employers in the Defense Department. The goal of von Braun's project was to launch an artificial satellite into orbit around the Earth by means of the Redstone rocket. The Defense Department passed the proposal along to the White House, where President Dwight D. Eisenhower turned it down. Eisenhower claimed it was wrong to use a weapon of war for a peaceful mission in space. Instead the president approved the development of the Vanguard, a new three-stage rocket proposed by the navy. The new spacecraft would be more suitable for the purpose of carrying a satellite

TECHNICIANS PERFORM A CONTROL CHECK OF THE JUPITER-C ROCKET ON NOVEMBER 1, 1957. THE ROCKET WOULD NOT BE USED THAT YEAR TO LAUNCH A U.S. SATELLITE BECAUSE PRESIDENT EISENHOWER DID NOT WANT TO USE A WEAPON OF WAR FOR A PEACEFUL MISSION.

into space, but it would have to be built from scratch. The deadline the government targeted was July 1957, the start of the International Geophysical Year (IGY). During this "year," which would actually end in December 1958, ten thousand scientists from more than sixty countries would work together to study and gain a better understanding of the Earth, its various environments, and outer space.

While the navy, with the help of von Braun and the army, was laboring on the Vanguard, Korolev in the Soviet Union was presenting his own proposal to Khrushchev. He wanted to send a satellite into space atop one of the new Soviet intercontinental ballistic missiles (ICBMs), rockets that can travel great distances. Khrushchev approved the plan, and Korolev worked night and day to prepare for a launch of an R-7 rocket. The R-7 was not a particularly powerful missile, but it proved ample for the task required. On October 1, 1957, the world was stunned by the news that the Soviets had sent *Sputnik*, the first artificial satellite into space. *Sputnik* is Russian for "satellite," and the date of its launch was less than a month after the one hundredth anniversary of rocketry pioneer Konstantin Tsiolkovsky's birthday.

Sputnik was a modest satellite by today's standards. It was a small steel ball less than 23 inches (58.4 centimeters) in diameter and

FLAMES AND SMOKE SIGNAL THE DISASTROUS END OF THE FIRST VANGUARD ROCKET LAUNCH AT CAPE CANAVERAL, FLORIDA, ON DECEMBER 6, 1957. NASA LEARNED FROM BITTER EXPERIENCE THAT DEVELOPING NEW ROCKETS FROM SCRATCH WAS TOO RISKY AND MADE IT IMPOSSIBLE FOR THE UNITED STATES TO KEEP PACE WITH THE SOVIETS IN THE SPACE RACE.

Animals in Space

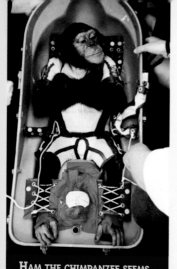

HAM THE CHIMPANZEE SEEMS UNAFFECTED BY HIS HISTORIC SPACE FLIGHT IN JANUARY 1961. HIS SUCCESSFUL FLIGHT CONVINCED NASA THAT THEY COULD SAFELY SEND A MAN INTO SPACE. FOUR MONTHS LATER THEY DID JUST THAT, AND ALAN SHEPARD BECAME THE FIRST AMERICAN IN SPACE.

Sending animals into space was a way for the Soviets and the Americans to test conditions and make sure space travel was safe for human beings. The Russians preferred dogs, which were intelligent and could be well trained. The United States favored monkeys and other primates because their body systems were closest to those of human beings.

On May 28, 1959, the United States sent two monkeys, Able and Baker, into space on a Jupiter rocket in two separate launches. They traveled to an altitude of 300 miles (483 kilometers) and returned safely to Earth an hour and a half later. Although they survived the journey with few ill effects, Able died a few days afterwards, probably from the effects of an anesthetic she was given before an electrode was removed from under her skin.

Following Laika's famed journey, the Soviets sent two female Samoyeds—Belka and Strelka—into space in *Sputnik 5* on August 19, 1960. They made seventeen orbits of Earth before returning safely in their capsule twenty-five hours later. When Strelka had a litter of puppies some time after, one was sent to U.S. president John F. Kennedy as a token of good will.

Perhaps the most remarkable animal astronauts, though, were two chimpanzees, Ham and Enos. They were trained to pull levers inside their capsule to help control its voyage. Ham was trained using electric shocks. Enos received a reward of banana pellets and water when he pulled his levers at the correct moment. During the flight, however, the circuitry failed, and Ham received shocks when he should not have. Nevertheless, the faithful chimp completed his tasks as he was supposed to and helped return his capsule to Earth.

weighing 184 pounds (84 kilograms). It was just large enough to hold a radio transmitter, a battery pack, and temperature sensors. Radiating from the satellite were four long flexible antennas to transmit radio signals. *Sputnik* orbited the Earth once every ninety-six minutes for a period of three months.

The success of *Sputnik* shifted the focus of cold war rocketry from defense to space exploration. The space race had begun, and the Soviet Union, to the shock and dismay of the Americans, was in the lead. The Vanguard had taken two and a half years to fully develop; Korolev had put together the launch of *Sputnik* in just six weeks. The Vanguard was finally ready for a test launch on December 6, 1957, from a military base in Cape Canaveral, Florida. It rose 3 feet (0.9 meter) into the air before exploding into flames.

A second attempted launch the following February also ended in disaster.

The Soviets, meanwhile, had established another first. Sputnik 2 carried the first living creature into orbit—a female dog named Laika—on November 3, 1957. The dog survived the takeoff and adjusted well to being in space, according to data sent to Earth from the satellite. The Soviets had no plan in place for the satellite's reentry, however, and Laika died after ten days in space when the oxygen in the satellite was used up.

Explorer I and the Birth of NASA

The failure of the first Vanguard launch had taught the Americans a valuable lesson. It was often better and more effective to use existing rocket models for space exploration than to spend more money and precious time developing completely new ones. Von Braun was finally given the official sanction to develop a satellite-launching rocket. He modified the Jupiter-C into a new rocket, the Juno-I. On January 31, 1958, Juno-I was successfully launched, carrying *Explorer I,* a satellite, into space.

Six feet ten inches (2 meters) in length, *Explorer I* weighed only 31 pounds (14 kilograms), about a sixth of the weight of the original *Sputnik.* However, its exploration of space proved more extensive than the Soviet satellite. Among the scientific instruments it contained was a detector that discovered rings of radiation surrounding the Earth. These rings were named the Van Allen Belts, after James Van Allen the scientist who led the team that designed the satellite instrumentation. Another seventy-eight *Explorer* satellites were launched from 1958 to 2000. The data and pictures they transmitted from space have greatly increased our knowledge of the universe.

Partially based on the success of *Explorer I*, President Eisenhower signed legislation in 1958 that established the National Aeronautics and Space Administration (NASA), the agency that would oversee and

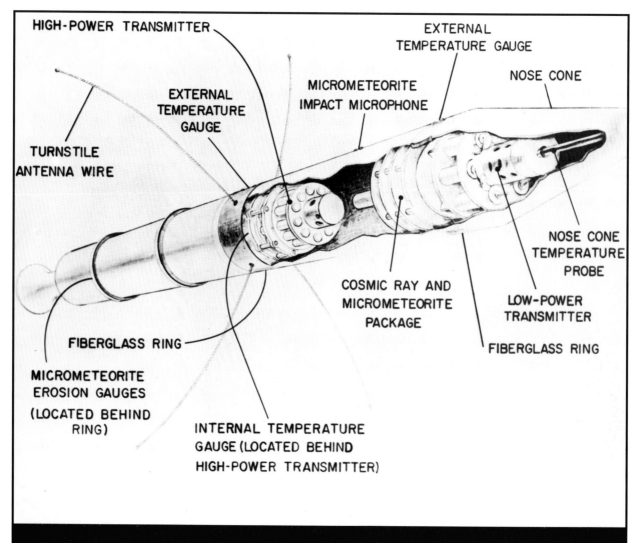

HIGH-POWER TRANSMITTER

EXTERNAL
TEMPERATURE GAUGE

NOSE CONE

EXTERNAL
TEMPERATURE
GAUGE

MICROMETEORITE
IMPACT MICROPHONE

TURNSTILE
ANTENNA WIRE

NOSE CONE
TEMPERATURE
PROBE

COSMIC RAY AND
MICROMETEORITE
PACKAGE

LOW-POWER
TRANSMITTER

FIBERGLASS RING

FIBERGLASS RING

MICROMETEORITE
EROSION GAUGES
(LOCATED BEHIND
RING)

INTERNAL TEMPERATURE
GAUGE (LOCATED BEHIND
HIGH-POWER TRANSMITTER)

THIS DIAGRAM OF *EXPLORER I*, THE FIRST U.S. ARTIFICIAL SATELLITE, SHOWS THE ATTENTION TO DETAIL AND TECHNOLOGY THAT WENT INTO ITS CONSTRUCTION.

run the U.S. space program. Its goal was "the expansion of human knowledge of phenomena in the atmosphere and space." Not surprisingly, Wernher von Braun was named the first director of NASA's flight center in Huntsville. Eisenhower deliberately set up NASA as a civilian agency, free of the military's control. By doing so, he sent a message to the world that the United States was exploring space in the cause of peace, and not war.

On October 7, 1958, NASA announced the start of Project Mercury. Its three goals were to place a manned spacecraft in orbital flight, investigate human performance capabilities in space and, perhaps most importantly, to see the safe and successful return of each mission sent. But once again, the Soviets would be the first in space.

THE SEVEN MERCURY ASTRONAUTS READY TO TAKE OFF FOR SPACE. THE BULKY SPACESUITS THEY WEAR WOULD LATER BE STREAMLINED AND MADE MORE PRACTICAL.

Travelers to the Stars

The requirements for the astronauts who would make up the Mercury team were stringent and very specific. Those men (women were not yet accepted) applying to be Mercury astronauts had to be younger than forty years of age, no taller than 5 feet 11 inches (1.8 meters), in top physical condition, and had to have perfect eyesight. They were also required to have worked as test pilots logging at least 1,500 hours of flying time, to belong to a branch of the military service, and have a bachelors of arts (BA) degree or its equivalent in engineering.

After a long search period, NASA announced in 1959 the seven members of the Mercury team. They were Alan Shepard, Virgil "Gus" Grissom, John Glenn, Malcolm Scott Carpenter, Walter Schirra, Gordon Cooper, and Donald "Deke" Slayton. All but Slayton would travel into space as part of the Mercury program.

Big Rocket, Cramped Capsule

The first two Americans in space would travel there in a small capsule mounted atop a Redstone rocket, a medium-range ballistic missile and a direct descendant of the V-2 rocket. The Redstone would carry the astronaut into space and then drop away, falling back into Earth's atmosphere, where it would disintegrate. The capsule would then continue on its own, traveling through space before eventually falling back to Earth.

The bell-shaped Mercury capsule was extremely small—less than 7 feet (1.9 meters) tall and only 6 feet (1.8 meters) wide. It had a control panel and just enough room for a specially made chair for the astronaut to sit in. The control panel was of little importance. The only control the pilot had during his journey through space was changing the altitude. While orbiting, he could not change the direction of the craft or do anything else. In nearly every sense, the Mercury astronauts were passengers, not pilots in space. The early models of the capsule did not even include a window for peering out into the vast reaches of space.

Perhaps the most significant feature of the capsule was the heat shield on the bottom of its exterior. As the capsule fell back into Earth's atmosphere, the friction of the capsule entering the atmosphere created tremendous heat. The thick heat shield would absorb this heat and prevent the capsule—and the astronaut inside—from burning up.

Once the capsule descended closer to Earth, a parachute would open, slowing the capsule's fall. NASA scientists had calculated the trajectory so the capsule would land or splash down into the open ocean, where a rescue crew would quickly recover both capsule and astronaut.

The First Men in Space

For nearly two years the seven Mercury astronauts underwent a rigorous training program to get them used to the intense gravity of blastoff and the weightlessness they would experience in the zero gravity of outer space.

Seven pilotless test rockets, two of them Redstones, were launched suborbitally. After four orbital test flights, a rocket was sent up in January 1961 with a chimpanzee named Ham on board. When Ham returned alive and well from space, NASA knew they were ready to send a human.

But as final preparations were being made, NASA and the entire world were stunned to receive news that a Soviet astronaut, called a cosmonaut, had already gone into space. On April 12, 1961, Yuri Gagarin, a

TWENTY-FIVE CENTS

APRIL 21, 1961

MAN IN SPACE

TIME

THE WEEKLY NEWSMAGAZINE

RUSSIA'S
YURI GAGARIN

$7.00 A YEAR

VOL. LXXVII NO. 17

THE FIRST MAN TO GO INTO SPACE, YURI GAGARIN IS HERALDED ON THE COVER OF THE APRIL 21, 1961, ISSUE OF *TIME* MAGAZINE. THE SOVIET COSMONAUT'S JOURNEY PUT TREMENDOUS PRESSURE ON U.S. SCIENTISTS TO GET THEIR OWN MAN INTO SPACE. GAGARIN TRAGICALLY DIED IN A PLANE CRASH SEVEN YEARS AFTER HIS HISTORIC FLIGHT.

twenty-seven-year-old army colonel, blasted off in a Soviet rocket *Vostok I* (*vostok* means "east" in Russian). As he orbited Earth, Gagarin radioed back that the planet had "a very beautiful sort of halo, a rainbow." Some 108 minutes after he blasted off, Gagarin returned to Earth, parachuting from his rocket about 4 miles (6.4 kilometers) above the surface.

While the Soviets claimed at the time that the mission had gone off without a hitch, years later a report was released that differed. On re-entry, *Vostok I* spun out of control and was in danger is crashing to Earth. Fortunately the capsule containing Gagarin separated from the rocket, just in time, and fell clear of it.

Once again the United States had been upstaged and embarrassed by the Soviets. Preparations were quickly made to send the first American astronaut, Alan Shepard, into space. The launch took place on May 5, 1961. The Redstone rocket that carried Shepard's capsule, *Freedom 7*, was not as powerful as the Russian rocket and could not lift the astronaut into orbit. As a result, Shepard's flight was suborbital and lasted only fifteen minutes twenty-two seconds.

Twenty days after Shepard's flight, the new president John F. Kennedy gave a new impetus to the Soviet space rivalry. "I believe this nation should commit itself to achieving the goal, before this decade is out, of landing a man on the moon and returning him safely to the earth," Kennedy declared in a speech before Congress. All subsequent NASA missions would have this ultimate goal in mind.

On July 21, 1961, Gus Grissom became the second American in space. This time there was problems. When his capsule *Liberty Bell 7* splashed down in the Atlantic Ocean, the hatch blew open and water gushed in, filling Grissom's space suit and pulling him down. A rescue crew got to him just before he drowned, but was unable to save the *Liberty Bell 7*. It became the only Mercury capsule not recovered after its mission.

While Grissom's voyage was also suborbital, the next Soviet in space, Gherman Titov, orbited the Earth for more than twenty-five hours. Titov, sent into space on August 6, 1961, racked up three more firsts. He was the first man to spend more than a day in space, the first to sleep in space, and the first to experience space sickness while weightless.

NASA knew that to catch up to the Soviets, the next American astronaut sent into space had to achieve orbit.

John Glenn, American Hero

For its February 20, 1962, Mercury launch, NASA used a more powerful rocket, the Atlas, the first successful ICBM. The historic flight began at 9:47 a.m. at Cape Canaveral. Abroad the capsule *Friendship 7* was astronaut John Glenn. The capsule rose 162 miles (261 kilometers) above the planet and circled Earth three times. Everything went smoothly until the second orbit. Signals from *Friendship 7* indicated to the command center that the heat shield was loose. Glenn tried to slow the capsule's re-entry and prevent it from burning up by releasing a retro-rocket affixed to the capsule. But when he saw chunks of burning metal streaming past his window, he feared that, despite his ef-

JOHN GLENN LOOKS CONFIDENT AS HE PREPARES TO BECOME THE FIRST AMERICAN ASTRONAUT TO ORBIT EARTH. THIS ACHIEVEMENT WOULD MAKE HIM A NATIONAL HERO.

forts, the entire capsule would be incinerated. Fortunately, the heat shield held up, and Glenn made it safely back to Earth.

The handsome, clean-living, and well-spoken Glenn became a national hero on his return. Huge parades were staged in his honor in Washington, D.C., and New York City, where he became the only astronaut to address the United Nations. Soon after Glenn left the space program and entered politics. After several disappointments, he eventually won a seat in the U.S. Senate, representing his home state of Ohio. In 1998, at age seventy-seven, John Glenn returned to space and became the oldest human to travel there as a member of the space shuttle crew.

THIRTY-SIX YEARS AFTER HIS FIRST HISTORIC JOURNEY, JOHN GLENN PREPARES TO MAKE A SECOND TRIP INTO SPACE ON A SHUTTLE MISSION. AT AGE SEVENTY-SEVEN AT THE TIME, GLENN PROVIDED SCIENTISTS WITH VALUABLE INFORMATION ON HOW AN OLDER INDIVIDUAL RESPONDS TO THE RIGORS OF SPACE TRAVEL.

There would be three more Mercury manned flights, all orbital. In May 1962, Scott Carpenter made three orbits around the Earth and barely had enough fuel to make it back home. Five months later, Walter Schirra flew six orbits and Gordon Cooper made 22.5 orbits in May 1963, becoming the first American to spend more than a day in space.

The Gemini Project

Project Mercury officially ended in May 1963. About a year later, Project Gemini, first announced in December 1961, began. It was named after the constellation that represents twin boys and was to be a bridge between the early manned space flights and flights aimed for the Moon. Like the constellation, the Gemini spacecrafts would carry two astronauts to work together to test the boundaries of what humans could achieve under the unique conditions of space.

Again, the Soviets took the lead. On October 12, 1964, they sent not two, but three, cosmonauts into space. In a flight the following March, Alexei Leonov became the first human to leave his spacecraft and "walk" in space for ten minutes.

Gemini 3, the first manned craft of the American project, was finally

PROJECT GEMINI PUT TWO ASTRONAUTS INTO SPACE IN THE SAME CAPSULE. THIS TITAN ROCKET CARRIED GUS GRISSOM AND JOHN YOUNG INTO SPACE ON MARCH 23, 1965.

ASTRONAUT ED WHITE WAS THE FIRST AMERICAN TO WALK IN SPACE, 120 MILES (193 KILOMETERS) ABOVE THE PACIFIC OCEAN DURING THE FLIGHT OF GEMINI 4.

launched on March 23, 1965. On board were Mercury astronaut Gus Grissom and newcomer John Young, one of nine newly recruited astronauts. For the first time, the astronauts had control over their flight. They could fire rocket motors to change the spacecraft's orbit. Later Gemini crews had simpler, easy-to-use controls that allowed them to perform re-entry and landing on their own as well as link up with other craft in space.

Gemini 3 remained in space for almost five hours, but two and a half months later, Ed White and James McDivett remained aboard Gemini 4 for four days. White left the craft attached to a tether and exercised for twenty-two minutes in what NASA called the first American extravehicular activity (EVA) in space.

Gemini 5, launched in August 1965, doubled the amount of time Gemini 4 spent in space. During the astronauts' eight days in space, Gordon Cooper and Charles "Pete" Conrad circled the Earth 120 times. Conrad had originally been expelled from the Mercury program when he complained about the numerous medical tests the astronauts had to undergo.

Linking Up in Space

Perhaps the greatest achievement of Project Gemini was realized in December 1965 when Frank Borman and James Lovell were launched aboard *Gemini 7*. Eleven days later, *Gemini 6*, manned by Walter Schirra and Thomas Stafford, joined them in space. At one point, the two spacecraft came within just 1 foot (0.3 meter) of each other, then flew in formation for more than five hours.

The first attempt to actually dock or join two craft in space nearly ended in disaster. Astronauts Neil Armstrong and David Scott, aboard *Gemini 8*, linked in space with an unmanned, medium-sized Agena rocket in March 1966. One of the *Gemini*'s thrusters became accidentally stuck in the "open" position, which caused the craft to spin wildly. The astronauts disengaged from the rocket, but were unable to restablize their craft. Armstrong finally managed to turn off the thrusters, and the craft made an early landing in the Pacific Ocean, half a world away from its scheduled landing place. Fortunately, NASA was able to track the craft, and the two astronauts were rescued.

Four more successful Gemini flights took place before NASA made final preparations for a lunar landing. The mission program was called Project Apollo after the Greek god of the sun, light, and truth. NASA scientists happily predicted that the lunar landing would take place as early as 1967, two years ahead of the final deadline established by President Kennedy. Kennedy was assassinated in November 1963 and would not be alive to see the historic event. But before the Apollo project could even get started, another unexpected tragedy took place that had dire consequences for the U.S. space program.

THIS DRAWING SHOWS THE SECOND STAGE OF THE *SATURN V* ROCKET BEING JETTISONED MINUTES AFTER LIFT-OFF AS THE APOLLO CRAFT CONTINUES ON ITS JOURNEY TO THE MOON.

SIX

To the Moon and Beyond

To reach the Moon, a much more powerful rocket was needed than in the orbital flights of projects Mercury and Gemini. None of the ICBMs, Wernher von Braun decided, had the power to send a capsule to the Moon or anywhere near it. On the other hand, he did not want to get bogged down again designing a new rocket like the Vanguard from scratch. So Braun and his team worked from the model of rockets that had already proved their merit, specifically the Redstone and the Jupiter.

The Mighty *Saturn V*

The rocket American scientists created, the *Saturn V,* was the largest and most powerful model built up to that time. When completed in 1966, it stood 363 feet (110.6 feet) tall, more than forty stories high. When loaded with fuel, supplies, and equipment, the *Saturn V* weighed more than 6 million pounds (2.7 million kilograms). This colossal three-stage rocket was the product of five years of labor by more than 325,000 workers.

The module that would ride atop *Saturn V* was unlike any capsule previously sent into space. As with the rocket, the capsule was composed of three separate units. The cone-shaped command module (CM) was where three astronauts would live as they traveled into space. A

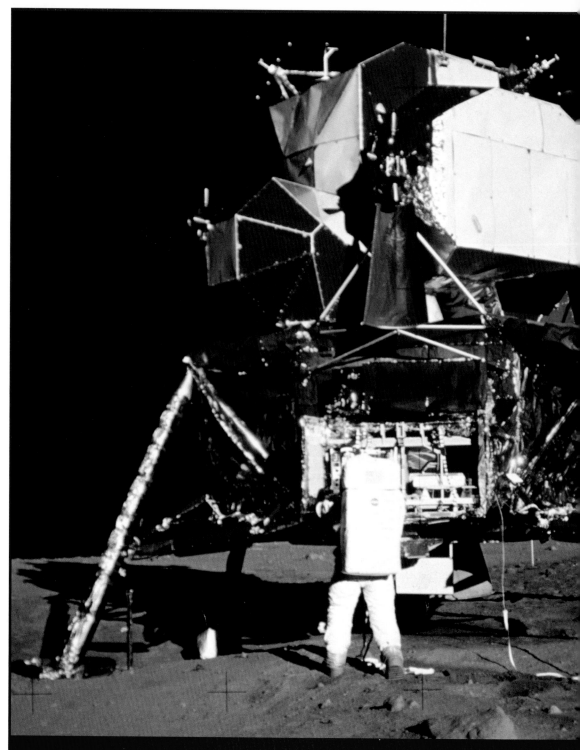

THE LUNAR MODULE SITS LIKE A GIANT INSECT ON FOUR SPINDLY LEGS ON THE MOON'S SURFACE.
BECAUSE OF THIS, IT WAS GIVEN THE NICKNAME THE BUG BY SCIENTISTS AT NASA.

small rocket in the front of the module could be used to guide the CM away from the rest of the craft in case of an emergency. The second main unit, the service module (SM), held the astronauts' equipment and supplies. Then the lunar module (LM) was located between the top of the launch rocket and the SM. After takeoff, the other launch rocket stages fell away, one by one, and the CM and SM separated as one unit from the LM. The combined CM and SM modules then inverted, and the LM attached to the front of the CM. Once in orbit near the Moon, two of the astronauts would enter the LM through a linking tunnel and from there access the lunar surface. NASA built fifteen complete sets of modules, twelve intended for manned flights and three for experimental unmanned flights.

Tragedy Strikes

Apollo 1 was scheduled to be launched in late February 1967. It would carry Gus Grissom, Ed White, and Roger Chaffee into orbit to test the module and its equipment. On January 27, the three astronauts entered the CM on the launching pad for a routine test. At 6:31 p.m., observers noticed a power surge on sen-

APOLLO 2 BLASTS OFF FOR THE MOON. THIS REMARK-
ABLE PHOTO WAS TAKEN WITH A TELESCOPIC CAMERA
MOUNTED IN AN AIR FORCE PLANE.

sors outside the CM. Moments later, Chaffee's frantic voice came over the intercom. "Fire, I smell fire," he said, then White cried, "Fire in the cockpit!"

Fueled by the pure oxygen in the module, the fire whipped through the enclosed space. By the time rescuers got into the module, all three men were dead from smoke inhalation and burns. It was the first loss of human life for the U.S. space program, and ironically the deaths occurred not in space but on the ground. Manned flights of the Apollo project were put on hold for nearly two years, while NASA employees investigated the tragic accident and went over every piece of equipment to make certain it would not happen again. They made a total of 1,500 modifications to the CM in that time.

Closer and Closer

On October 11, 1968, *Apollo 7,* the first manned mission, was finally ready to be launched. Walter Schirra was the commander, assisted by Donn Eisele and Walter Cunningham. The rocket that carried them into space was not the *Saturn V* but a smaller version, the *Saturn IB.* The crew orbited the planet for eleven days testing out a new guidance system before returning safely to Earth.

Apollo 8 went a step further in December 1968, going beyond the Earth's orbit to orbit the Moon. *Apollo 9* was less ambitious, but also significant. It orbited the Earth, where the crew tested the LM in space for the first time. *Apollo 10* returned to the Moon's orbit, and once there two of the crew traveled in the LM within just 9 miles (15 kilometers) of the lunar surface, but had orders not to land there. When *Apollo 10* returned safely to Earth, NASA decided the next mission would be the one to actually land on the Moon.

"One Giant Leap for Mankind"

Neil Armstrong, Edwin "Buzz" Aldrin, and Michael Collins were the three astronauts chosen by NASA for the historic *Apollo 11* mission. They blasted off from Cape Kennedy, Florida, on July 16, 1969. Four days later, their craft was poised above the surface of the Moon. Armstrong and Aldrin rode the lunar module to the Moon's surface, while Collins stayed in the command module.

ASTRONAUT BUZZ ALDRIN WALKS ON THE MOON'S SURFACE AT TRANQUILITY BASE.

At 10:56 p.m. Eastern Daylight Time (EDT), Armstrong stepped down from the last rung of the lunar module and onto the Moon's surface. "That's one small step for a man, one giant leap for mankind," he said via radio to the hundreds of millions of people back on Earth watching the drama unfold live on television, broadcast from a camera strapped to one of the legs of the lunar module.

Fifteen minutes later, Aldrin joined his partner on the lunar surface, which they described as covered with powdery grains. "It has a stark beauty all its own," said Armstrong of the Moon's landscape. "It's like much of the high desert of the United States."

For the next couple of hours, the two astronauts were busy. They planted an American flag on the Moon's surface, conducted science experiments, and collected rock and soil samples. They also talked via radio with President Richard Nixon. Before they returned to the command module they left a plaque behind that read: "Here men from the planet Earth first set foot upon the Moon, July 1969 AD. We came in peace for all mankind." Commenting on the Moon landing, Esther Goddard, the widow of Robert Goddard, said that the event was the fulfillment of her husband's dream. "He would just have glowed," she told reporters.

Apollo's Final Missions

The six remaining Apollo flights were somewhat anticlimactic but added greatly to the world's knowledge of the Moon and the capabilities of the rockets and modules. *Apollo 12* landed on the Moon and continued the work begun by *Apollo 11*. Charles Conrad, one of the shortest astronauts, amended Neil Armstrong's historic statement, when he became the third man to walk on the Moon. "Whoopie!" he exclaimed. "Man, that may have been a small one for Neil, but that's a big one for me." The astronauts collected more samples from the lunar surface and conducted a host of science experiments for nearly eight hours. The next mission, *Apollo 13,* would be less fortunate and nearly end in disaster.

Alan Shepard, the first American in space, was part of the *Apollo 14* flight. During his more than nine-hour stay on the Moon, Shepard hit a golf ball. With little gravity to slow it, the ball traveled for miles along the lunar surface. The program had far surpassed the expectations of even the most ambitious NASA engineers. With the return of *Apollo 17* from its 1972 mission, NASA officially brought Project Apollo to an end. The agency had planned several more manned flights, but a cutback in funding and general public indifference had altered their plans. As of 2007, humans have not returned to the Moon.

Labs in Space

While the Americans were exploring the Moon, the Soviet space program was floundering. In April 1967 the Soviet space agency launched a powerful new rocket called the *Soyuz 1*,

The Ill-Fated Flight of Apollo 13

The superstitious among NASA workers wanted the organization to skip over thirteen in numbering their missions. While NASA ignored the requests, *Apollo 13* indeed proved to be unlucky.

On April 13, 1970, yet another occurrence of the number, fifty-six hours into the flight, a crewmember stirred the tanks of liquid oxygen, not knowing that one tank's wiring was faulty. The stirring shorted the wire, and a fire broke out. The heated gas burst the tank, and the resulting shortage of oxygen made it impossible for *Apollo 13* to continue to the Moon. Instead, the astronauts, led by their commander Jim Lovell, began the return trip to Earth with dangerously low supplies of water, oxygen, and electricity. They journeyed in the lunar module, which had its own undamaged life-support systems, and for the next four days lived on 6 ounces (0.18 liter) of water a day. As they neared Earth, the astronauts returned to the command module for the final re-entry. They splashed down in the Pacific Ocean and were then flown to Honolulu, Hawaii. They were dehydrated and suffering from hypothermia due to the cold temperature inside the module, but alive. In 1994 Jim Lovell published a book about the hair-raising experience, *Lost Moon*. A year later the book was transformed into the hit movie *Apollo 13*, directed by Ron Howard and starring Tom Hanks as Jim Lovell.

APOLLO 15 LIFTS OFF AT CAPE CANAVERAL ON JULY 26, 1971. ON THIS MISSION, THE LUNAR ROVING VEHICLE WAS FIRST USED, ALLOWING ASTRONAUTS TO EXPLORE MORE OF THE MOON'S SURFACE THAN ON PREVIOUS MISSIONS.

(meaning "union"), which rivaled *Saturn V*. On its first orbital flight, the parachute system became entangled on re-entry and the craft crashed to Earth, killing the lone cosmonaut aboard, Vladimir Komarov.

In January 1969 the cosmonauts aboard *Soyuz 4* and *Soyuz 5* docked in space and changed vehicles, accomplishing the first crew transfer in space. In April 1971 *Soyuz 10* met a floating, unmanned Soviet laboratory in space. When the two craft docked, they created the world's first space station, the *Salyut 1* (meaning "salute"). But, again, tragedy followed triumph. The three-man crew of *Soyuz 11* was on its way home after twenty-four days at the space station in June 1971 when a valve malfunctioned and released all the air from their module. All three cosmonauts died of suffocation.

In 1973 NASA followed the Soviet's lead and built its own space station with the equipment left over from the remaining Apollo modules. Called *Skylab*, the huge cylindrical craft became the largest object in space to date. *Skylab* had room for three astronauts to live and work. Between May 1973 and February 1974, three crews of astronauts docked at the space station and resided there for up to two months at a time.

Working Together in Space

The last Apollo spacecraft was sent into space as part of a joint mission with the United States's longtime cold war enemy. On July 15, 1975, *Soyuz 19* was launched with two cosmonauts abroad. Just seven hours later, *Apollo CSM-111*, with its three astronauts, was sent into orbit. Once in space, it used an attached docking module to link up with *Soyuz*. The Americans boarded the Soviet craft and shook hands with their Russian counterparts as millions on Earth watched via live television. Over the next two days, the two teams worked together performing experiments in the space station.

LOOKING LIKE A STRANGE HELICOPTER IN SPACE, *SKYLAB 3*'S COMMAND MODULE SOARS OVER EARTH. IT WAS THE LARGEST HUMAN-MADE OBJECT IN SPACE TO THAT TIME.

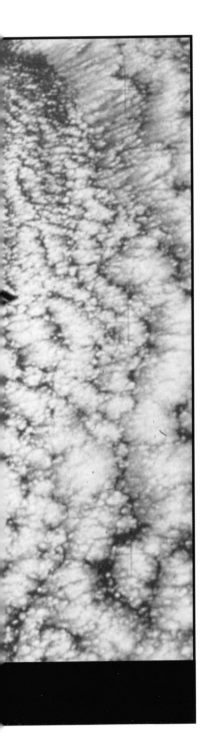

It was a shining hour in the history of space exploration. Although the cold war stretched into the 1980s, Americans and Soviets joined forces in space for a peaceful purpose to benefit both their countries and the world. If there was any doubt that the future of rockets lay in scientific exploration and not in warfare, this historic moment quickly dispelled it.

SPACE WORKERS PROUDLY ACCOMPANY THE SPACE SHUTTLE *Atlantis* TO THE VEHICLE ASSEMBLY BUILDING ON JULY 22, 2005, WHERE IT WAS MOUNTED WITH ITS EXTERNAL TANK AND SOLID ROCKET BOOSTERS BEFORE ITS SEPTEMBER LAUNCH.

Seven

Space Shuttles and Space Stations

Up until the early 1970s, the goal of the U.S. space program was to make more and more powerful rockets to take humans beyond Earth's atmosphere and to the Moon. But once humans had landed on the Moon, the agency's goals and objectives changed. Building huge rockets for space travel had become exorbitantly expensive. Manned missions to other planets—such as Mars—was, at the time, beyond NASA's capabilities. The exploration of space and how humans could operate and function in this still largely unknown environment became NASA's primary focus. NASA envisioned building a permanent space station above the Earth, where scientists could live and work for long periods of time. An inexpensive and reusable kind of rocket was necessary to transport people to and from this scientific outpost. So the engineers looked first to creating rockets and modules that could be returned to Earth in working order and be used over and over again.

The Space Shuttle

The craft that NASA came up with was the space shuttle. Part rocket and part airplane, the shuttle was composed of three sections. The central segment, the orbiter, was made up of living and work areas for the astronauts aboard, the engines that powered the craft, and a sizable cargo bay. It could be launched like any other manned rocket, sent into orbit, and when ready to return, glide without fuel back to Earth and make a soft horizontal landing, much like an airplane, on a specially made 3-mile-long (4.8-kilometer) runway.

The shuttle's second component was two booster rockets strapped to the sides of the orbiter. These gave the craft the extra thrust it needed to leave Earth's atmosphere. The boosters would jettison from the orbiter a little more than two minutes into the flight. Parachutes would be activated to slow their descent, and the units would splash down into the Atlantic Ocean where they would be safely retrieved by two ships. The third component was an external fuel tank also strapped to the orbiter. It would remain on the shuttle for about six minutes. At that time, it would have spent all its fuel and jettison from the orbiter as well. It would be the only part of the shuttle that would be used only once. As it descended rapidly, the tank would disintegrate in Earth's atmosphere.

Development of the space shuttle began in earnest in 1972. The first unmanned shuttlecraft made its debut four years later. It was named the *Enterprise* in honor of the fictional starship that explored the universe in the popular 1960s science-fiction television series *Star Trek*. The *Enterprise* was first launched, piggybacked on a jumbo passenger jet, on June 18, 1977, and made a successful suborbital flight.

The *Columbia* Takes Off

The next important step was to launch a manned shuttle with two astronauts. This craft, the *Columbia,* underwent several test flights before being readied for launching on April 10, 1981. The launch was delayed two days. Coincidentally, it left the ground exactly twenty years to the day that Soviet cosmonaut Yuri Gagarin became the first human to be sent into space.

The shuttle was piloted by astronauts John Young and Robert Crippen who were blasted into orbit 170 miles (274 kilometers) above

THE SPACE SHUTTLE *COLUMBIA* IS SEEN ON ITS FIRST LAUNCH IN APRIL 1981. THE REUSABLE SHUTTLES WOULD SAVE NASA BILLIONS OF DOLLARS OVER THE YEARS.

Two and half months before they met their deaths in the *Challenger* tragedy, the seven crewmembers pose for a photo. Teacher Christa McAuliffe is second from the left in the top row. Mission commander Dick Scobee is in the center of the bottom row.

Earth. They returned two days later, making a safe landing at Edwards Air Force Base in California.

After such a successful test run, the *Columbia,* and later three more space shuttles—*Challenger, Discovery,* and *Atlantis*—made regular flights into space. Each one seemed to set a new record or achieve another first in space. In June 1983, thirty-two-year-old Sally K. Ride became the first American woman and the youngest American astronaut in space. (The Soviets had sent female cosmonaut Valentina Tereshkova into space twenty years earlier.) As a mission specialist for the *Challenger,* Ride helped transport two communications satellites into space. This was to become an important job for the shuttles for years to come.

Two months after Ride's voyage into space, mission specialist Guion Bluford became the first African American in space. His *Challenger* mission was the first to take off and land at night. Bluford would make three more flights. Then in November 1983, the shuttle carried a complete laboratory, *Spacelab,* into orbit, another first. Aboard this mission was Franklin Chang-Diaz, the first Latino American astronaut, serving as orbit capsule communicator.

The *Challenger* Tragedy

The next major accomplishment for the space shuttle program was sending a civilian into space. President Ronald Reagan wanted the first civilian astronaut to be an effective communicator and decided a teacher would best fulfill that role. Some 11,500 teachers applied for the position and Christa McAuliffe, a high school social studies teacher from Concord, New Hampshire, was the one chosen. After months of training, McAuliffe prepared for takeoff with six other astronauts on what was to be the *Challenger*'s tenth voyage into space. By then, the space shuttle had become a rather routine event for the public, and the media barely took notice. That all changed however on the morning of January 28, 1986. Less than one second after liftoff, black smoke was visible billowing from the spacecraft. A little more than a minute later, the *Challenger* exploded in midair. All seven people aboard perished.

The *Challenger* disaster was one of the darkest days in the history of the U.S. space program. For the first time Americans had died in flight, an event shown live on television to millions of horrified viewers. A thorough investigation later revealed that the O-rings that strapped the fuel tank to the orbiter had been faulty. The cold temperatures on the morning of the launch had caused the rings to weaken and come loose. The solid rocket booster broke away from the fuel tank, rupturing it in the process. The tank, in turn, leaked liquid hydrogen that fed the flames coming out of the booster rocket. This caused part of the *Challenger*'s wing to break off. The orbiter went into a free fall, disintegrating in space.

Blame for the unforeseen tragedy rested squarely on NASA's shoulders. Officials there had become careless in their rush to get the space shuttle aloft. Several engineers warned that the O-rings were a potential problem the morning of the takeoff, but officials ignored them. For the next two years, shuttle flights were suspended. Thousands of modifications were made, among them an escape system for the crew.

A Soviet Space Shuttle

When the shuttle program was resumed with the launch of *Discovery* in 1988, it proved once again to be a success. Over the next decade, sixty-seven shuttle missions were flown. Among their accomplishments were the delivery and retrieval of satellites and probes and the repairing of satellites in space.

At the same time that the United States was exploring space with its various shuttles, the Soviets were building one of their own. Their VKK *Buran* ("Snowstorm") was similar to the American space shuttles, but with some significant differences. Instead of attached boosters and an external fuel tank, their craft had an enormous liquid-fuel booster rocket, the *Energiya* ("Energy"), carrying the shuttle into space. About 197 feet (60 meters) tall, it was the largest and most powerful rocket to date. Like the United States–built boosters, the *Energiya* was meant to drop back to Earth, with the help of parachutes, to be retrieved and used again and again.

Exploring the Universe: Unmanned Probes

Since the 1980s the space shuttle has launched numerous manned space probes that have explored nearly every corner of the solar system and sent back to Earth valuable photographs of what they have seen.

Among the most significant of NASA's probes is Galileo, launched from the space shuttle *Atlantis* in 1989. Galileo reached Jupiter, the largest planet in the solar system, in 1995 and sent back thousands of spectacular images of Jupiter's rings, its moons, and other features, many of which had never been seen before.

Equally as important is the Hubble Space Telescope (HST), sent into space aboard the shuttle *Discovery* in 1990. Flaws in its mirror lens prevented the HST from functioning until astronauts from the space shuttle *Endeavor* boarded and repaired it three years later. In the years since, the HST had taken photographs of distant galaxies and innumerable stars at various stages of their evolution. It even discovered 1,500 ancient galaxies in a corner of the universe previously thought to be empty.

NASA is not the only space agency to launch probes. The European Space Agency (ESA) launched Giotto in 1985, the first probe to fly directly into the center of Halley's comet to photograph it. Four years later, ESA launched Hipparcos, which measured the position and motion of more than 100,000 stars.

Pluto was until recently the only one of the nine planets not explored by a space probe. On January 19, 2006, the probe New Horizons was launched by NASA. It is scheduled to arrive in Pluto's atmosphere in 2016 and record images of the planet and its largest moon, Charon. "The New Horizons mission is going somewhere no mission has gone before," said project scientist Hal Weaver. "This is the frontier of planetary science."

On November 10, 1988, an unmanned *Buran* was launched into orbit and successfully returned to Earth. Despite this initial success, the *Buran* never took to the skies again. Escalating economic and political problems in the Soviet Union ended their space shuttle program. The Soviet Union dissolved as a political entity on December 25, 1990.

Other nations, including Great Britain, France, and Japan, conceived of space shuttles of their own, but none was ever built. The enormous cost of development and construction was too much of a burden for any one of these countries to take on by itself.

Stations in Space

The Soviet Union was more successful in creating a space station where rockets and other spacecraft could dock and astronauts could conduct valuable research. The Soviet space station *Mir* (meaning "a community liv-

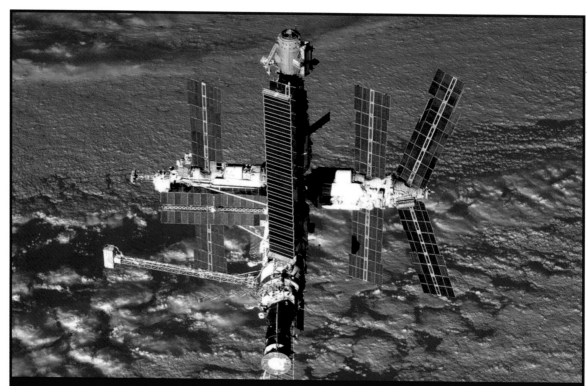

THE RUSSIAN SPACE STATION MIR IS SEEN IMMEDIATELY AFTER UNDOCKING FROM THE SPACE SHUTTLE *ATLANTIS* IN SEPTEMBER 1996. THIS PICTURE WAS TAKEN FROM THE SPACE SHUTTLE.

ing in harmony") was launched in February 1986 and until March 2001, when it fell into the Pacific Ocean, was almost continually occupied by a crew of astronauts. The compact but efficient *Mir* consisted of four main areas—a docking compartment with six rocket ports; living quarters; a work area; and a propulsion chamber to hold the station's rocket motors, fuel supply, and heating system. To allow the space station to communicate with Earth, antennas are attached outside the propulsion chamber.

The United States' plan for a space station, to be called *Freedom,* was not successful. *Freedom* was abandoned as too expensive by the government in the early 1990s. Instead, the United States took advantage of the already operational Russian space station, sending astronauts there to work with their Soviet cohorts. American astronaut Shannon Lucid spent six months on *Mir* beginning on March 23, 1996. This was the longest amount of time a U.S. astronaut has spent in space to date. Perhaps equal to Lucid's accomplishment was the return to space in 1998 of one of the first American astronauts, John Glenn.

The Oldest Astronaut

Ever since he became the first American to orbit the Earth, John Glenn had wanted to return to space. In January 1998, he finally got his chance and became, at age seventy-seven, on a shuttle flight launched on October 29, 1998, the oldest person to be sent into space. With six other astronauts, Glenn spent nine days in space, orbiting the Earth 134 times. That was 131 more orbits than on his first flight back in 1962.

On his return, Glenn underwent a battery of tests for three weeks at the Johnson Space Center in Houston, Texas, to evaluate the effects of space and weightlessness on his aging body. More tests on muscles and bones were conducted over the next six months. The information scientists gained from Glenn's experience will prove invaluable in the future, as more and more Americans of every age and size get the opportunity to travel into space.

"I got great satisfaction the first time out of just being up there and being the first one to do this for our country," Glenn said after his second journey into space. "And here I am all these years later."

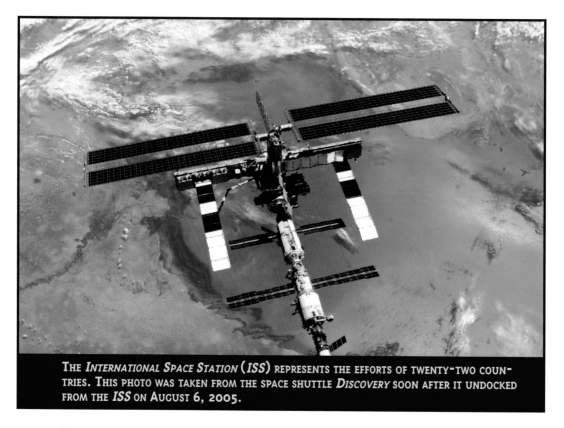

THE *INTERNATIONAL SPACE STATION* (*ISS*) REPRESENTS THE EFFORTS OF TWENTY-TWO COUNTRIES. THIS PHOTO WAS TAKEN FROM THE SPACE SHUTTLE *DISCOVERY* SOON AFTER IT UNDOCKED FROM THE *ISS* ON AUGUST 6, 2005.

The *International Space Station*

Mir served as a model for a new and bigger space station that would be the result of a joint effort on behalf of several nations. The *International Space Station* (*ISS*) grew out of the failed plans for *Freedom* and was a way for the United States to share the financial burden of such an ambitious project with other countries. These partners include Russia (the largest part of the former Soviet Union), Japan, Canada, Italy, Brazil, and the European Space Agency (ESA), whose seventeen members include the United Kingdom, Ireland, Portugal, Austria, and Finland. Work on the *ISS* began in 1995 with all country members contributing funding and expertise. Since 2000 a team of three astronauts has continually been living and working on *ISS*.

About 356 feet (109 meters) across and 290 feet (88.4 meters) long, the *ISS* weighs more than a million pounds (453,592 kilograms).

It orbits Earth at an altitude of 220 miles (354 kilometers), where it can be easily reached by rockets and spacecraft from the various member countries. Solar panels on the station's exterior produce enough electrical power to run the six science laboratories housed there. When finally finished, perhaps in 2007, the *ISS* will have a rotating team of six scientists aboard at any given time. Their main areas of inquiry will be learning the way humans, animals, and plants adapt to life in space and the nature of space itself.

The *ISS* may be the beginning of the fulfillment of the dream of having people live in space that was first put forth by Konstantin Tsiolkovsky and Hermann Oberth more than eighty years ago. It is the next modest stage of human endeavor in the vast, mysterious universe.

THIS RUSSIAN *SOYUZ* TMA-2 ROCKET IS DRAMATIC PROOF THAT THE INTERNATIONAL SPACE PROGRAM IS STILL ALIVE AND WELL, DESPITE RECENT SETBACKS. AN AMERICAN ASTRONAUT AND A RUSSIAN COSMONAUT RODE THE ROCKET TO THE NEWLY BUILT *INTERNATIONAL SPACE STATION* (ISS) ON APRIL 26, 2003.

Rockets of the Future

On January 14, 2004, President George W. Bush delivered a speech to NASA employees in which he called for a renewal of the U.S. space program and a return to the exciting days of the Mercury and Apollo missions. He set goals for a return to the Moon, the establishment of a lunar base, and a manned mission to Mars. He challenged NASA to "extend a human presence across our solar system."

The president's words were inspiring, but met with a less than enthusiastic response. Americans had not forgotten that less than a year earlier the United States had experienced its worst disaster in space since the *Challenger* tragedy seventeen years earlier.

The *Columbia* Disaster

By the start of the twenty-first century, the U.S. space program had fallen on hard times. With the collapse of the Soviet Union and the end of the cold war the rivalry that once drove the space race was gone, and NASA had found no new incentive to replace it. Public opinion cooled regarding the space program. Congress, faced with other national priorities, reduced NASA's budget. The organization had to make do with far fewer funds at its disposal. Yet the shuttle program continued to move forward, with safety often taking a backseat to efficiency.

On January 16, 2003, the space shuttle *Columbia* lifted off in what appeared to be a textbook launch. NASA officials breathed a long sigh of relief, for the mission had been delayed thirteen times over a two-year period, once after the discovery of cracks in the shuttle's propellant system. After the liftoff, NASA officials examined a film of the launch and were dismayed to see that a piece of foam insulation had broken off from the external fuel tank about eighty-two seconds into the flight. It appeared to have struck the shuttle's left wing, but it did not seem to be a hazard to the craft when it reached orbit.

On the morning of February 1, the *Columbia* was returning to Earth when disaster struck. The breach in the wing proved more serious than initially suspected and caused the shuttle to break apart in the intense heat of re-entry. The entire craft disintegrated soon after as it soared over Texas. All seven crewmembers perished.

A thorough investigation of the tragedy revealed the fallen foam was the immediate cause. The investigative report went on to say that a culture of negligence and recklessness at NASA was equally responsible. All plans for future shuttle launches were cancelled, and in his January 2004 speech President Bush called for the eventual retirement of the remaining shuttle crafts by 2010, the projected date for completion of the *International Space Station*. The question on many Americans' minds was what would replace the twenty-five-year-old space shuttle? What rockets of the future would take astronauts safely into the renewed exploration of space?

Rise of the Rocketplanes

In the early 1990s, the rocket of the future looked to be as much airplane as traditional rocket. While the space shuttle landed horizontally like a traditional airplane, these new hybrids would take off in a similar fashion, soaring into space as a complete one-stage entity, not comprised of two or three stages, like earlier rockets. These spacecraft came to be called single stage to orbit (SSTO) craft.

One such SSTO, the National Aero-Space Plane (NASP) or the X-30, developed by NASA and the Defense Department, looked like a supersonic jet, but traveled much faster. A special engine called a scramjet that ran on hydrogen boosted its speed to thousands of miles per hour.

Even more impressive was the X-33, developed by Lockheed Martin, a private company. This wedge-shaped rocket looked and acted like a giant wing. Other private companies were busy developing their own "rocketplanes" and trying to obtain a government contract to manufacture them. In 1996 NASA awarded a contract to build the X-33 to Lockheed over two other competitors. The agency planned to develop this rocketplane, grooming it to become the successor to the space shuttle. But after five years of intensive development that cost Lockheed and NASA close to a billion dollars, the project was cancelled and the X-33 abandoned because it was found to be too expensive and impractical for the space program.

The concept of a rocketplane, however, remained viable. Burt Rutan, designer of the *Voyager,* the first aircraft to fly around the world without refueling, came up with the SpaceShip One (SSO), a squid-shaped craft

SPACESHIP ONE, THE FIRST COMMERCIAL MANNED SPACESHIP SOARS OVER CALIFORNIA'S MOJAVE DESERT PRIOR TO ITS FIRST OFFICIAL LAUNCH ON JUNE 21, 2004. SINGLE STAGE ROCKETS LIKE THIS ONE MAY SOON BE CARRYING ORDINARY PEOPLE INTO SPACE AS TOURISTS.

and another single stage to orbit vehicle. Nine years in the making, SSO was lifted into the skies on the belly of a carrier airplane over California's Mojave Desert on September 29, 2004, on its second flight. At an altitude of 50,000 feet (15.2 kilometers), the SSO detached from the mother craft and climbed another 300,000 feet (91 kilometers) to an altitude of about 64 miles (103 kilometers) above Earth, the very edge of space. The pilot then returned to Earth, gliding down to a landing on a runway. The SSO became the first privately developed craft to take a human into space. On October 4, Rutan and SpaceShip One received the prestigious Ansari X Prize, a $10-million purse awarded as part of an international competition to encourage the building of spacecraft by private commercial companies.

Space Tourism

Why would private companies such as Lockheed Martin, Boeing, and Microsoft, which helped Rutan finance his SpaceShip One, go into the risky business of rocket building in the first place? The answer is space tourism. A far-fetched idea only a short time ago, space tourism since the 1990s has been seen as a reality in the near future and a growth industry that many companies want to be a part of. The first space tourist was multimillionaire American Dennis Tito, who paid $20 million in 2001 to go up in the Russian *Soyuz* to the *International Space Station.* The following year South African Mark Shuttleworth paid the same amount to make the same trip, becoming the first African in space. The next space tourists, however, will pay far less for a trip into space. Rutan has joined forces with British airline owner Richard Branson, whose new company Virgin Galactic hopes to take up to five people at a time on suborbital flights in SpaceShip One by 2008. The cost? $200,000 per person. Space Adventures, another company started in Virginia in 1997, has already taken deposits of $10,000 from a number of people for pending space flights.

While these space tourists may not get to the Moon anytime soon, they will be able to gaze on the Earth from outer space and feel the ef-

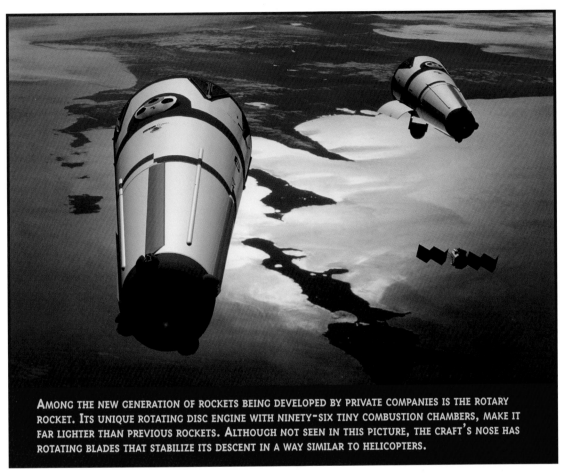

AMONG THE NEW GENERATION OF ROCKETS BEING DEVELOPED BY PRIVATE COMPANIES IS THE ROTARY ROCKET. ITS UNIQUE ROTATING DISC ENGINE WITH NINETY-SIX TINY COMBUSTION CHAMBERS, MAKE IT FAR LIGHTER THAN PREVIOUS ROCKETS. ALTHOUGH NOT SEEN IN THIS PICTURE, THE CRAFT'S NOSE HAS ROTATING BLADES THAT STABILIZE ITS DESCENT IN A WAY SIMILAR TO HELICOPTERS.

fects of weightlessness on board their spacecraft. Once the exclusive domain of rugged, professional astronauts, space may soon be visited and enjoyed by ordinary people with the money to pay for it. And beyond that, rockets may carry people to other planets, to explore and eventually colonize them. However, traveling these long distances will take a much bigger and more powerful kind of rocket.

Back to the Future

While rocketplanes may be a viable way to take tourists for short trips into space, NASA has returned to the tried and true roots of its past in shaping its own future in space. In August 2005, it unveiled its long-awaited design for its next rocket program—the Crew-Exploration Vehicle (CEV). It resembles nothing so advanced and futuristic as the old Apollo capsule. The payload, whether cargo or human beings, will be

A Rocket to Mars

The exploration of Mars by U.S. astronauts had been proposed as far back as the late 1940s when Wernher von Braun devised a plan to send no less than ten giant spaceships to the red planet. The proposal was rejected as impractical, and in 1969, the year of the first Moon landing, von Braun came up with a more viable plan for one spaceship, powered by nuclear power. It did not get past the drawing board either.

The problem with reaching our nearest planetary neighbor in space is the great distance. While the Moon is only four days away for the Apollo spacecraft, a rocket trip to Mars would take an estimated ten months. And then the ship would have to return to Earth, which would take another ten months. The key to shortening that time is a faster rocket with more efficient fuel.

In 2000 the Advanced Space Propulsion Laboratory at the Johnson Space Center unveiled the Variable Specific Impulse Magnetoplasma Rocket, better known as VASIMR. Its engine uses radio waves to heat fuel to a high degree in order to make it more powerful. This high-temperature fuel could potentially destroy the engine it is feeding, but scientists have eliminated this problem by using magnetic fields to guide the hot plasma out of the rocket's rear. The fuel boosts the rocket's speed to 650,000 miles (1,046,074 kilometers) per hour and could cut the flying time to Mars, from ten months to four.

A manned mission to Mars is still years away, but when it happens it may well be the VASIMR, or some variation of the rocket, that carries it there.

THIS RENDERING SHOWS THE LAUNCH OF VARIOUS CREW VEHICLES CAPABLE OF LONG-DISTANCE SPACE TRAVEL.

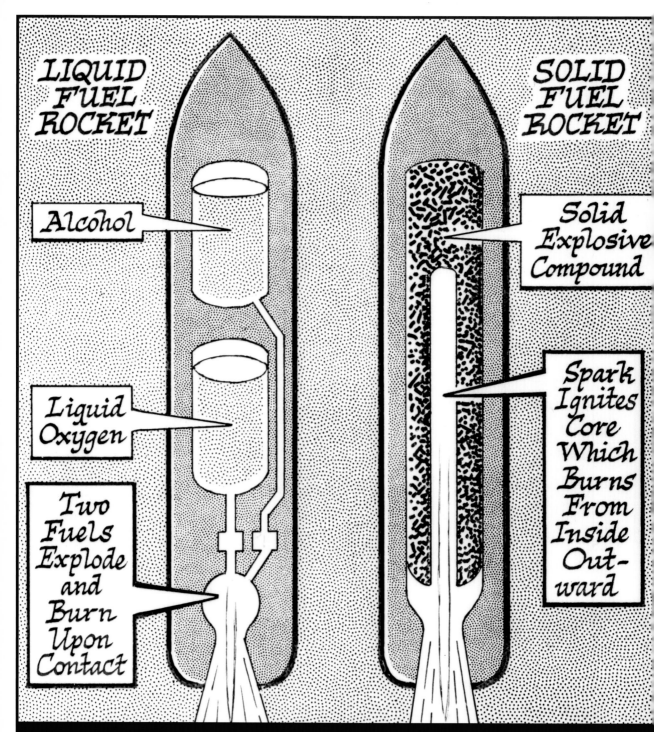

LIQUID FUEL ROCKET

SOLID FUEL ROCKET

Alcohol

Liquid Oxygen

Two Fuels Explode and Burn Upon Contact

Solid Explosive Compound

Spark Ignites Core Which Burns From Inside Outward

THE SCIENCE OF ROCKETS HAS COME A LONG WAY SINCE THE DAYS OF THE SIMPLE MODELS OUTLINED IN THESE DIAGRAMS. ADVANCES IN DESIGN AND FUEL EFFICIENCY MAKE FLIGHTS TO ONCE-DISTANT REACHES OF THE UNIVERSE WITHIN THE REALM OF POSSIBILITY.

perched atop the rocket in a capsule, as with the Mercury spacecraft, far removed from the dangers of the rocket engine and the potential debris that has caused so much trouble in the past for the space shuttles.

NASA has designed two kinds of rockets to carry the CEV—the larger of the two will be 350 feet (107 meters) tall and be able to carry six times the cargo weight as the shuttle. The smaller rocket will be 184 feet (56 meters) high, still bigger than the shuttle, and be designed with the three modules of the Apollo craft. One day it will take humans to the Moon and perhaps even other planets, beginning with Mars. This CEV will be ten times safer than the shuttle and will be equipped with an escape system to lift the capsule out of danger in case of an emergency.

Ironically, both these rockets will be built largely with parts from the shuttle. This will make them cost efficient but still safe and reliable. NASA has already set goals of sending the CEV to the *International Space Station* by 2011 and to the Moon by 2018.

Despite the setbacks and disappointments of the past, the space program continues. The future looks exciting as new rockets take astronauts farther than ever before in the exploration of space, and average citizens get the opportunity to experience the thrill of blasting off into space. Like the dreamers, designers, and pioneering astronauts of the past, many of us long to burst the bonds of Earth and see the wonders of the universe. If and when we do, you can be sure that it will be a rocket that will take us there.

about 400 B.C.E.
Applying the principle of action and reaction, Greek inventor Archytas invents a "flying" wooden pigeon, applying a principle integral to rocketry.

about 62 C.E.
Greek inventor Hero of Alexandria creates a spinning ball using the same principle.

about 600–1000
The Chinese create the first gunpowder-based war rockets.

1232
The Chinese use rockets to drive the Mongols from the city of Kai-fung-far.

1379
Rockets are documented for the first time in Europe at the siege of Chioggia in Italy.

1780
The British are introduced to rocket warfare by the Indians at the battle of Pollilur in September.

1804
Englishman William Congreve publishes *A Concise Account of the Origin and Progress of the Rocket System.*

1807
Congreve's rockets are used by the British to decimate Copenhagen,
Denmark.

1814
American Francis Scott Key writes of "the rockets' red glare" as the
British bombard Fort McHenry in Baltimore Harbor on September 13
during the War of 1812.

1846
English inventor William Hale creates a more accurate war rocket by replacing the guide stick with vanes.

1903
Russian Konstantin Tsiolkovsky publishes "Investigation of Interplanetary Space by Means of Rocket Devices," which lays the groundwork for
modern rocketry.

1907
American Robert Goddard builds his first experimental rocket.

1923
Hermann Oberth publishes *The Rocket into Interplanetary Space.*

1926
Goddard launches the first liquid-propellant rocket on March 26.

1927
The Society for Space Travel (VfR) is founded in Breslau, Germany.

1929
A rocket trip to the Moon is realistically depicted in Fritz Lang's film
Woman in the Moon.

1931
Johannes Winkler launches the first successful liquid-fuel rocket in Eu-

rope on March 14; the German Army forms a department of rocket research to develop war weapons.

1942
The German rocket department, under Wernher von Braun's direction, successfully launches the A-4 rocket on October 3.

1944
The A-1, renamed the V-1 rocket, is used to attack England, beginning in June; the German rocketeers produce the V-2 rocket, which is launched by the thousands against England and Antwerp, Belgium, beginning in September.

1949
The Bumper-Wac, a redesigned V-2 rocket, is launched by the United States with the help of German scientists on February 24.

1956
The Army Ballistic Missile Agency (ABNA) is established at Huntsville, Alabama.

1957
The Soviets launch *Sputnik,* the first artificial satellite sent into space on October 1; *Sputnik 2* carries Laika, a dog, the first living creature in space on November 3; the U.S. Vanguard rocket fails in its test launch on December 6.

1958
The United States sends *Explorer I,* the first U.S. satellite into space on January 31; the United States establishes the National Aeronautics and Space Administration (NASA) to operate its space program; Project Mercury, a manned space mission, is announced on October 7.

1959
The seven astronauts of Project Mercury are officially introduced on April 9.

1961
Soviet cosmonaut Yuri Gagarin becomes the first human in space on April 12; U.S. astronaut Alan Shepard becomes the first American in space on May 5; Cosmonaut Gherman Titov orbits the Earth for more than twenty-five hours on August 6–7.

1962
Astronaut John Glenn becomes the first American to orbit the Earth in his capsule *Friendship 7* on February 20.

1964
Three Soviet cosmonauts go into space on October 12.

1965
Gus Grissom and John Young make up the first dual American flight team in space on March 23; *Gemini 6* and *Gemini 7* meet in space in December.

1967
Three astronauts, including veteran Gus Grissom, die in an accidental fire inside their module during a routine test on January 27.

1968
Apollo 7, the first manned mission of this Moon project, takes off with three astronauts aboard on October 11.

1969
Neil Armstrong and Buzz Aldrin are the first humans to step onto the Moon on July 20.

1970
The *Apollo 13* mission is forced to abort its trip to the Moon and return to Earth in April in the nearest disaster in U.S. space program history.

1971
The Soviets create the world's first space station, *Salyut I*, when *Soyuz 10* meets an unmanned Soviet lab in space in April.

1973
NASA sends *Skylab,* a space station, into space where it is visited by a crew of three astronauts in May.

1975
The astronauts of *Apollo CSM-111* and the cosmonauts of *Soyuz 19* rendezvous in space from July 15 to 17.

1977
The first space shuttle, the *Enterprise,* makes a successful suborbital flight.

1981
The first manned space shuttle, the *Columbia,* remains in space from April 12 to 14.

1983
Sally K. Ride becomes the first American woman in space in June; Guion Bluford becomes the first African American in space in August.

1986
Six astronauts and schoolteacher Christa McAuliffe perish moments after takeoff in the space shuttle *Challenger* on January 28; the Soviet space station *Mir* is completed in February.

1988
The Soviets launch the space shuttle *Buran* for the first and only time on November 10.

1995
Six space agencies begin work on the *International Space Station (ISS).*

1996
Astronaut Shannon Lucid begins a six-month stay on *Mir* working with Soviet cosmonauts on March 23; NASA gives a government contract to Lockheed Martin for its X-33, a rocketplane.

1998
Astronaut John Glenn becomes, at age seventy-seven, the oldest person in space aboard the space shuttle *Discovery* from October 29 to November 6.

2000
The Advanced Space Propulsion Lab unveils the VASIMR, a high-speed rocket possibly capable of taking astronauts to Mars.

2001
NASA cancels its contract with Lockheed Martin, and the X-33 is abandoned.

2003
The space shuttle *Columbia* disintegrates on re-entry, killing all seven crewmembers on February 1.

2004
President George W. Bush delivers a speech declaring a renewed space program on January 14; designer Burt Rutan's SpaceShip One makes a successful test flight on September 29.

2005
NASA announces the Crew Exploration Vehicle (CEV), a new rocket that will replace the space shuttle after 2010.

2006
The unmanned probe New Horizons is launched on January 17 bound for Pluto.

2007
The *International Space Station* (*ISS*) is scheduled to be completed.

artificial satellite—A human-made craft designed to orbit a body in space, usually for exploratory or communications purposes; it is distinct from a natural satellite, such as the Moon which revolves around the Earth.

astronaut—A person trained to fly or navigate a rocket or other spacecraft.

booster—A rocket used to give another craft the power needed for takeoff, such as the solid-fuel rockets attached to the space shuttle.

capsule—A small craft to carry astronauts into space, usually positioned atop a larger rocket.

cosmonaut—A Soviet or Russian astronaut.

European Space Agency (ESA)—An intergovernmental agency devoted to space exploration that was established in 1975 and currently has seventeen members including the United Kingdom, Ireland, Portugal, Austria, and Finland.

extravehicular activity (EVA)—A special activity that is performed by a person in space outside his or her capsule or module, such as a walk in space or linking up with other spacecraft.

intercontinental ballistic missile (ICBM)—A powerful rocket that can travel great distances and whose path is determined solely by the pull of gravity and air friction.

liquid-fuel rocket—A rocket that runs on liquid fuel such as liquid oxygen and liquid hydrogen; it is more powerful and more controllable than a solid-fuel rocket.

module—A spacecraft for astronauts to live and work in that is larger and more advanced than a capsule; modules can also hold supplies and equipment and serve as craft to land on another body such as the Moon.

multistage rocket—A rocket that is made up of smaller rockets that detach as their fuel is used up.

National Aeronautics and Space Administration (NASA)—The government agency that oversees the U.S. space program, founded in 1958.

orbit—(noun) The path that an object follows when traveling around another object.

orbit—(verb) To move around an object, such as a planet or other celestial body.

orbiter—The part of the space shuttle that carries humans.

payload—The cargo carried in a rocket or other spacecraft.

propulsion chamber—A section of a space station such as the Russian *Mir* that holds rocket motors, fuel supply and a heating system.

rocket—A flying object that is propelled by the reaction to the force of the gases being released out of its back or rear.

rocketplane—A rocket designed to take off and land horizontally like an airplane.

solid-fuel rocket—A rocket fueled by solid material or a powder; it is simpler and less expensive than a liquid-fuel rocket, but also less powerful and less capable of being controlled in flight.

sounding rocket—A rocket used for atmospheric research.

space shuttle—A rocket designed to carry people and cargo into space and back that can be used again and again.

SSTO (single stage to orbit)—A rocket that can escape the Earth's gravity in one piece, without extra stages that hold fuel and are later discarded in space.

suborbital—A flight into space that does not escape Earth's gravity and that does not go into orbit around the Earth or Moon.

thrust—The force that pushes a rocket.

vane—A small metal blade in the exhaust nozzle of a rocket that, if placed at an angle, can make the rocket spin as it moves.

Verein fur Raumschiffahrt (VfR)—The first rocket society in Germany, founded in 1927, from which came many leading German rocket scientists and designers.

V-2 rocket—A highly destructive rocket used in warfare by the Germans against the British and their Allies during World War II.

Brief History of Rockets
http://quest.arc.nasa.gov/space/teachers/rockets/history.html

Human Space Flight
http://spaceflight.nasa.gov/home/index.html

National Association of Rocketry
http://www.nar.org/

Robert Goddard
http://www.nasa.gov/centers/goddard/about/dr_goddard.html

Books

FOR STUDENTS

Ashby, Ruth. *Rocket Man: The Mercury Adventure of John Glenn.* Atlanta: Peachtree Publishers, 2004.

Clay, Rebecca. *Space Travel and Exploration.* New York: Twenty-first Century Books, 1997.

Miller, Ron. *The History of Rockets.* New York: Franklin Watts, 1999.

Spangenburg, Ray, and Diane K. Moser. *Wernher von Braun: Space Visionary and Rocket Engineer.* New York: Facts on File, 1995.

Younkin, Paula. *V-2 Rockets.* New York: Crestwood House, 1994.

FOR TEACHERS

Benjamin, Marina. *Rocket Dreams: How the Space Age Shaped Our Vision of a World Beyond.* New York: Free Press, 2003.

Chun, Clayton K.S. *Thunder over the Horizon: From V-2 Rockets to Ballistic Missiles.* Westport, CT: Praeger Security International, 2006.

Clary, David A. *Rocket Man: Robert H. Goddard and the Birth of the Space Age.* New York: Hyperion Books, 2003.

Englebert, Phillis, and Diane L. Dupuis. *The Handy Space Answer Book.* Detroit: Visible Ink Press, 1998.

Gruntman, Mike. *Blazing the Trail: The Early History of Spacecraft and Rocketry.* Reston, VA: American Institute of Aeronautics and Astronautics, 2004.

Winter, Frank H. *The First Golden Age of Rocketry: Congreve and Hale Rockets of the Nineteenth Century.* Washington, D.C.: Smithsonian Books, 1990.

Page numbers for illustrations are in **boldface**.

About the Author

Steven Otfinoski has written more than 120 books for young readers. His many biographies include books about Jesse Jackson, Oprah Winfrey, John Wilkes Booth, Nelson Mandela, and Boris Yeltsin. He has also written books on geography, world history, rock music, public speaking, and writing.

He is the author of *Marco Polo: To China and Back, Francisco Coronado: In Search of the Seven Cities of Gold, Vasco Nuñez de Balboa: Discoverer of the Pacific, Juan Ponce de León: Discoverer of Florida,* and *Henry Hudson: In Search of the Northwest Passage* in the Great Explorations series. His other works for Marshall Cavendish include the twelve-volume transportation series for early readers Here We Go! and books on New Hampshire, Georgia, Maryland, and Washington State in the Celebrate the States and It's My State! series.

Two of his books, *Triumph and Terror: The French Revolution* and *Poland: Nation in Transition,* were chosen as Books for the Teen Age by the New York Public Library.

Otfinoski is also a produced playwright and has his own theater company History Alive! that brings plays about American history to schoolchildren. He lives with his wife, Beverly, and their two children in Connecticut.